AS BAD AS THEY SAY?

AS BAD AS THEY SAY?

Three Decades of Teaching in the Bronx

JANET GROSSBACH MAYER

Empire State Editions

An imprint of Fordham University Press

New York   2011

Fordham University Press has no responsibility for the persistence or accuracy of
URLs for external or third-party Internet websites referred to in this publication
and does not guarantee that any content on such websites is, or will remain,
accurate or appropriate.

Fordham University Press also publishes its books in a variety of electronic
formats. Some content that appears in print may not be available in electronic
books.

Library of Congress Cataloging-in-Publication Data

Mayer, Janet Grossbach.
    As bad as they say? : three decades of teaching in the Bronx / Janet Grossbach
Mayer.
        p.   cm.
    Includes bibliographical references and index.
    ISBN 978-0-8232-3416-5 (cloth : alk. paper)
    ISBN 978-0-8232-3417-2 (pbk. : alk. paper)
    ISBN 978-0-8232-3418-9 (ebook : alk. paper)
    1. Mayer, Janet Grossbach.   2. High school teachers—United
States—Biography.   3. English teachers—United States—Biography.
4. Teaching—New York (State)—New York.   5. Bronx (New York, N.Y.)
I. Title.
LA2317.M367   2011
373.110092—dc22
[B]
                                                              2010052426

Printed in the United States of America
13 12 11   5 4 3 2 1
First edition

To the memory of my beloved son
Jeffrey Charles Mayer
Who passed away while I was writing this book
(October 10, 1964–September 22, 2007)
He fought the good fight.

Contents

Part III: Losing Our Way

Appendixes

Foreword

At a time of crisis and upheaval in the New York City school system, when tests, assessments, and school closings have left students and teachers feeling battered and demoralized and when leadership of the system has been handed from a prosecutor to a magazine executive, perhaps people concerned with education should begin listening to voices like Janet Mayer's. Mayer, the author of *As Bad as They Say? Three Decades of Teaching in the Bronx*, wrote her book not only to highlight the heroism of Bronx high school students and teachers in the face of poverty, violence, and shockingly decayed and understaffed schools but also to denounce the educational reforms that have come out of Washington in the past ten years, which, Mayer feels, have made matters much, much worse. Among the many critics of the two great national education initiatives, No Child Left Behind and Race to the Top, Mayer stands out for embedding her critique in a detailed portrait of teaching and learning in one of the nation's poorest urban school districts. No one has ever written more eloquently than Janet Mayer about what it takes to spend a large portion of your career teaching children in poverty. Those who read *As Bad as They Say?* will be inspired by her stories of fortitude and creativity on the part of students and teachers, but they will also come away enraged that voices like hers have been marginalized in the debate over how to improve America's schools. Veteran teachers like Janet Mayer are the forgotten moral compass in America's educational reform movement. We ignore what she says at our peril.

Mayer's arguments have a special resonance with me because of the experiences I have had organizing workshops, lectures, and neighborhood tours for Bronx teachers for the research project I direct, the Bronx African American History Project. During the past seven years, I have spent time in more than thirty Bronx high schools, elementary schools, and middle schools and have come away from the experience incredibly impressed by the dedication and creativity of the teachers and administrators I have met, many of whom were, like Mayer, products of Bronx public schools themselves. These educators, put under immense pressure to raise their students' test scores lest their schools close and their jobs be placed in jeopardy, still found the time to use the information we presented to organize displays, performances, plays, and festivals that celebrated community history, often involving students, parents, and grandparents to help with the research. Their dedication made a tremendous impression on me, and when Janet Mayer came to me with an early draft of her memoir, I saw an opportunity to give a whole generation of underappreciated Bronx teachers and principals a voice.

As you begin reading *As Bad as They Say?*, prepare yourself for a view of teaching and teachers that is radically different from the contemptuous one often put forward by educational reformers, business leaders, and print and broadcast media. Janet Mayer grew up in a time, the late 1940s and early 1950s, when working-class New Yorkers revered teachers and were proud when their children decided to make teaching their career. Janet Mayer came from such a family, and becoming an English teacher in the New York public schools was the fulfillment of a lifelong dream. She started teaching middle school in 1960, when she was twenty-one years old, and nearly quit several times because the job was so difficult; but with the support of family members and her own tireless efforts to discover new ways of helping students appreciate literature, she became a highly successful English teacher in a largely white public high school in the northeast Bronx. Mayer's almost legendary popularity in that school derived from a few key things—her ability to get students excited about reading and writing by creating an electric atmosphere in her classroom supplemented by individualized assignments for students, and her willingness to defend students and colleagues against the excesses of an authoritarian and vindictive principal who ruled the school with an iron hand. Mayer approached these twin missions as a sacred calling, working long hours into the night and on weekends, protected in her efforts by that much-maligned institution the United Federation of Teachers, the union that had become the official bargaining agent for New York City teachers in the 1960s. Because the UFT had proven its power in several long strikes, Mayer points out, teachers could demand better treatment for students and for themselves without getting fired, something Mayer demonstrated by filing grievance upon grievance against her principal and even bringing his conduct to the attention of the superintendent of New York City schools and to the New York State Labor Relations Court of Law.

Finally, in frustration at the Board of Education's refusal to remove her principal despite massive evidence of irresponsible conduct, Mayer decided to transfer to another Bronx high school, this one a vocational high school with a nearly 100 percent black and Latino student population. It is Mayer's experience at this school—whose identity she hides by calling it "Carter High School"—that inspires the major storyline of *As Bad as They Say?* The working conditions at Carter High School almost defy description. Elevators don't work. Windows don't open. Textbooks are missing. Classrooms are so filled with mice that teachers have to scream when they enter to scatter the vermin! Teachers' bathrooms are filthy and never have toilet paper, while student bathrooms are unusable. Crack vials fill the schoolyard, which has been turned into a teachers' parking lot; gunshots periodically ring out in the street outside the school. Teachers who park there risk having their cars vandalized or stolen. And for Carter students, conditions are worse. There are too few guidance counselors for the more than 1,800 students at the school. Except for a three-year period when the school got a grant, there were no elective music or art classes, because most music and art teachers in the city had been fired during the fiscal crisis of the mid-1970s. The students who came to Carter were, for the most part, children of immigrants or products of the Bronx's poorest, most troubled families. Many of them were at Carter because they couldn't get into any other school.

And yet Janet Mayer loved teaching there! In *As Bad as They Say?* she explains why—because for many of the students she worked with, it took heroic efforts even to come to school, much less pass courses and graduate. Using real-life stories, with names that have been changed, Mayer explains what these students are up against. Parents murdered. Families evicted. Apartments without heat and hot water—for years. Pregnancies. Debilitating illnesses. Language problems as a result of recent arrival in the country. Work responsibilities, as often a student was his or her family's only wage earner. Fear of coming to and from school, or even walking through the hallways lest they be set upon by bullies or thugs. Reading and math levels more appropriate for fourth- and fifth-graders than for high school students. And in the face of all these things, the students persevere, with the help of teachers like Janet Mayer, and on more than a few occasions manage to graduate from high school and go on to college, in some cases ten or fifteen years after they first entered the high school.

As Bad as They Say? not only tells several stories of triumph over adversity, it reveals what a great teacher does to help such students succeed. Teaching, Janet Mayer–style, is a 24/7 job. Let us see how she gets students with fourth- and fifth-grade reading levels to pass English and in the process learn to love reading, She creates folders filled with magazine articles on subjects students are interested in—ranging from sports, to dance, to space exploration—to get students to improve their reading skills and enjoy reading inside and outside of class. She tutors students after school to help them pass regents tests. She creates a new course, called Multicultural Literature, to help students of color and those from multiple cultural backgrounds see their experiences reflected in materials they are given to read. She starts a letter exchange with a high school in South Africa, in the years following apartheid, wherein the South African students all ask their Carter counterparts, "Is the Bronx really as bad as they say?" And she is available at all hours, on weekends as well as weekdays, to help students deal with life-changing issues, from helping them find homes when they are homeless, to finding counselors when they have emotional problems, to helping them gain access to music or dance or theater when the school doesn't provide it, to helping them visit and choose colleges. And that involvement inspires lifetime loyalty. Janet Mayer's students are her students for life, still asking for advice or just keeping in touch twenty-five to thirty years later and showing appreciation for having had faith in them when life seemed to present so many problems.

How do you assess this kind of teaching? How do you measure it? How do you grade it? The answer is, of course, you can't, and when the federal government, shortly after Mayer retired, passed No Child Left Behind, which required school districts and schools to meet arbitrary standards of performance, Mayer was both enraged and deeply suspicious. She was enraged because she knew that neither student learning nor great teaching can be easily quantified, as much of it involves emotional growth, life lessons, and the unleashing of creativity; she was suspicious because she believed that when test performance becomes the sole criterion upon which schools are evaluated and teacher salaries and job tenure are determined, statistics can and will be manipulated. Mayer's final chapter, a devastating critique of business-driven education reform models currently in favor in Washington and New York City, begins with a chilling description of how the landmark federal education initiative No Child Left Behind was based on allegedly revolutionary results achieved in the Houston public schools that, future studies revealed, *were based entirely on bogus data*. The chapter ends with a critical analysis of mayoral control of New York City schools that among other things points out that Bloomberg administration claims of dramatic improvements in test scores and graduation rates were achieved only by "dumbing down" state tests and that greater success was achieved meeting national standards before mayoral control than after. It also points out that the closing of large high schools and their replacement with small schools, something that Mayer had familiarity with as a teacher mentor in ten Bronx high schools, often created mass chaos in school buildings where it took place and left young teachers without the guidance of department chairs and assistant principals that typically helped new teachers adjust under the old system.

By the time you finish reading *As Bad as They Say?*, you may well become convinced, as I am, that putting businesspeople in charge of public schools may have been the single worst policy decision of the twenty-first century and that performance assessments devised by American business are not to be trusted (think of the Triple A ratings given packages of sub-prime mortgages from Moody's and Standard and Poor's!).

But even if you don't agree with everything Janet Mayer says about No Child Left Behind, Race to the Top, and mayoral control of New York City public schools, you cannot help but be moved by her portrait of the heroism of her Bronx students and the life-changing power and extraordinary dedication displayed by great teachers. At the very least, after reading *As Bad as They Say?*, you will insist, in the strongest possible language, that teachers like Janet Mayer be given a place at the table when school reform is being discussed. It is through the efforts of teachers like Janet Mayer, inside and outside the classroom, that the lives of students are transformed.

Dr. Mark Naison
Professor of African American Studies and History, Fordham University; co-author of Allen Jones's *The Rat That Got Away: A Bronx Memoir*

Nobody can make it out here alone

Many indispensable people helped, guided, and encouraged me throughout the writing of this book. My husband, Larry, my muse, is, as always, at the top of my list of ardent, invaluable, and influential supporters. Nothing is possible without him! My son Stuart and daughter-in-law Maureen—my electronic media specialists who unraveled every snafu, of which there were many—gave countless hours of their time to patiently reading my manuscript and offering suggestions. I also made full use of Maureen's prodigious editing skills and truly appreciate her unfailingly prompt responses as deadlines approached. Stuart's and Maureen's suggestions were always thoughtful and insightful, and I couldn't have completed this book without them. My granddaughters, Sarah and Rachel, have always helped me by making me laugh, keeping me young, and just being themselves. My "Precious" brother Allan, who passed away in 2009, relentlessly urged me to write this book.

My very dear friends and colleagues Iris Tolksdorf and Jacqueline Goldstein not only lived through and shared most of my school adventures and events, but they also sat with me for incalculable hours, in numerous half-empty restaurants and fast-food courts, and listened tirelessly and attentively to my readings of each chapter. They gave generously of their time, experience, and advice, and the feedback I received from them was enormously helpful. Their support and encouragement and, most of all, their friendship will always be treasured.

The title of this section is from Maya Angelou's poem *Alone*.

Speaking of lasting friendships, my childhood girlfriend from the Bronx, Rosalind Alcana, my kindergarten partner more than sixty-seven years ago, has always appreciated my work as a teacher and has had great faith in my ability to write this book and make a difference. I value and hold in the highest esteem her loyalty, her confidence in me, and our lifelong friendship.

My cousins Bob and Sylvia Grossbach were there from the beginning, giving graciously of their time and experience. The advice and suggestions given by cousin Bob, an author himself, were practical and priceless, and I will forever appreciate them.

On the journey toward publication, I will always be grateful to Dr. Jeffrey Ravel, a professor of history at MIT, who heard about my book from my son Stuart (they are longtime college friends) and introduced me to his colleague Dr. Craig Wilder, also a professor of history at MIT, who, coincidentally and serendipitously, is a Bronxite like me. He, in turn, kindly introduced me to Dr. Mark Naison, professor of African American studies and history at Fordham University and director of the Bronx African American History Project. It is to Dr. Naison that I owe the most profound, everlasting gratitude. He met with me and encouraged me to expand upon my original manuscript. Without his promptings and powerful, provocative suggestions, this book never would have evolved into what it is today. I am extremely appreciative of all the time and consideration he gave to the reading and promoting of my book, and I am forever in his debt.

It was through Dr. Naison's efforts that Fordham University Press read my manuscript and agreed to publish it. Special thanks to Fredric Nachbaur, director of the Press, and Eric Newman, managing editor. I am also very grateful to Teresa Jesionowski, the book's copy editor, and the rest of the staff at Fordham University Press for their tireless efforts on my behalf.

As you can see, I never could have made it out here alone.

To the Reader

The students I have written about in this book really do exist, and the crucial moments in their lives that I have described are accurate to the best of my memory.

To protect everyone's privacy, I have disguised the names of all the students and faculty and the two Bronx high schools where I taught.

AS BAD AS THEY SAY?

I

Bronx Roots

1
Introduction

September is—for me—the most beautiful month of the year. Here in the Northeast part of the United States, the weather is near-perfect, not too hot and not too cold. The autumn leaves are in all their glory, and so am I. I have spent sixty-one of my seventy-one Septembers in a New York City classroom, beginning as a kindergartner and ending as a teacher. I guess that you can say that I never got out of school, and since most of my years in the classroom were spent in the Bronx, I guess you can say that I never got out of the Bronx; but then again I never really wanted to.

In September 1944, after completing my very first day of kindergarten, I ran home from school (parents didn't wait anxiously outside for their children then) to my family's rented four-room apartment on Boynton Avenue in the Bronx and announced to my at-home mother (as most mothers were) that I had had a sensational day. I told her that when I grew up, I was going to be a teacher. My destiny was truly decided that day. Eight years later, in June 1952, when I graduated from P.S. 77 in the Bronx and received the award for Best Student in English, my career path was crystal clear: I would become an English teacher.

In a hurry to begin my chosen career, I was very focused. I rushed through school, graduating in three and one-half years from high school in January 1956 and graduating from Queens College, New York, in January 1960. In between, in 1958, I married my childhood sweetheart—now my lifelong sweetheart.

In order to become a New York City high school teacher in the 1950s and 1960s, one had to pass a series of pedagogical, scholastic, cultural, and teaching proficiency tests. These tests were usually given twice a year, once in the spring and once in the fall. Graduating in January placed me too late for the fall exam and too early for the spring one. My college advisor arranged for me to take a special exam in January, with the promise of a teaching position in February, if I passed.

There was a wicked snowstorm on the scheduled exam day in January. I boarded the New York City subway, headed for Brooklyn Technical High School, where all exams were given. But the train didn't move; I sat anxiously and impatiently, for over an hour, only to hear an overhead announcement that all New York City trains were shut down indefinitely, not for terrorist threats in those years, but because of a massive snowfall that blocked all the elevated tracks. First I cried; then I got off the train and called home—no cell phones then. Despite my tears, I was able to hear my mother's calming advice: "Call Brooklyn Technical High School and explain." I did that, and the person I reached was aware of the trains' shutdown and promised to hold the exam for me, until whatever time I arrived, which was six hours later. I remember thinking, "Years from now, Janey girl, you will laugh about this critical day in your life," but I wasn't laughing then, that's for sure.

Two weeks later, I was notified that I scored high and was going to be appointed to my first school on February 1, 1960. My childhood dream was about to be fulfilled.

That first year of teaching was incredibly difficult. The second year was also incredibly difficult. In fact, all the forty-four years that I was a New York City teacher were incredibly difficult, but they were also personally and professionally satisfying beyond my wildest expectations.

The years flew by; my family grew; I had two fine sons; and I continued teaching in New York City.

In 1994, through the auspices of the American Federation of Teachers, my Bronx high school students were matched with South African high school students in a classroom-to-classroom pen-pal program. I corresponded with Dr. Mahomed Hoosen Rasool, a high school teacher, from KwaZulu/Natal, South Africa. He was kind enough to send me information about South Africa and the ending of apartheid education in 1995. He wrote that under apartheid "there was no semblance of a normal school life [for his students]. Political violence, state harassment, poverty and other social ills have ensured that the academic development of black children remained retarded; however, with the inauguration of a democratic order in South Africa, teachers have the mighty task of uplifting disadvantaged children from formerly disenfranchised communities. With this in mind, I am sure that your students will understand and accept the many shortcomings of my pupils brought on by three hundred years of systematic racial persecution." (See Appendix A for the entire letter.)

I gave all of this information to my students as they prepared to write their first correspondences. I cautioned them to be prepared to receive very interesting but perhaps poorly written letters.

There was great excitement in my class the day the first batch of letters arrived. I gave every student a letter, and each one read his or her letter out loud. To my astonishment, and to my students' astonishment, almost all of the letters, legible and literate, by the way, asked the same question: "Is the Bronx as bad as they say?"

I was born in the Bronx, grew up in the Bronx, and had been teaching there, at this point, for more than twenty years. I saw my students as my heroes, who, despite overwhelming obstacles, were not only capable of high achievement but, more important, were also outstanding human beings. Over the years, they taught me—a cliché, but nevertheless true—more than I could have ever taught them, and then and there I made a promise to this class that when I retired ("Oh, no, Mrs. Mayer, you can never retire"—music to my ears—"when you are too old to walk, we will carry you from classroom to classroom"), I would write a book about them so that the whole world could learn that Bronx students, contrary to what others may believe, contrary to expectations, were young people of remarkable character, unlimited potential, uncommon courage, and indomitable will.

Throughout the 1990s and until 2005, when I finally did retire from New York City schools, having commuted for my last three years from Pennsylvania to the Bronx every day, I continued to tell each class that I was going to write a book about them. I reminded them to display exemplary behavior so as not to embarrass themselves or me when their stories appeared in print.

Over all these years, it has been an honor as well as a privilege to have taught more than fourteen thousand students, a staggering number! I have chosen to highlight a small representative number of Bronx students who passed through my classroom and my life. It would take many books to tell all their stories, but I hope that readers will learn from these profiles what Bronx high school students are like, and to see them as I do:

real, but unsung, heroes in our society. They may not be rock stars or basketball icons or movie idols; they are just young people who taught me, every day, how to live, by their examples of extraordinary courage, deep pride, soaring spirits, and unbelievable tenacity. These attributes should count for a lot in life, maybe even everything. Unfortunately, these qualities are not measured by any standardized tests, nor should they ever be.

This book is dedicated to my Bronx students and to all urban students across America who not only have had to endure very difficult home problems but also have had to overcome abysmal school conditions that were beyond their control (see Chapter 3, "It Was the Worst of Times"). They were (and still are) subjected to overcrowded classrooms, decaying buildings, and grossly underfunded schools. New York City waited for thirteen years, beginning in 1993, to receive $4.7 billion more a year owed to them as a result of New York State landmark court decisions stating that "its financing system denied city students the opportunity to get a sound, basic education."[1]

Also, "When you look at the cumulative deprivation of resources over time, it's not surprising that you end up with dropout rates of forty percent or higher . . . and New York's high school graduation rate ranks fortieth in the nation and near last for minorities."[2]

I regret to have to tell you that after waiting for thirteen years, New York City did not receive the needed funds. On November 21, 2006, the New York State's highest court "ended a landmark legal case over education financing, ruling that at least $1.93 billion more must be spent each year in New York City's public schools—far less than $4.7 billion that a lower court called the minimum needed to give city children the chance for a sound basic education."[3]

City councilman Robert Jackson is quoted as saying, "I am profoundly distressed and disappointed. . . . The children of New York City are crying in their hearts."[4] And I'm crying too!

In the No Child Left Behind Act of 2002 (NCLB), the federal government was supposed to improve failing schools, but just like New York State, it has not provided adequate funding to do the job. In addition, NCLB was supposed to guarantee a highly qualified teacher (i.e., one with a college degree) in every classroom by 2005;[5] however, not one school district in the country has met that standard at this writing. NCLB does not even address the quality of administrators. Do they not have to be qualified?

In case the above-mentioned financial obstacles to the education of our city's youth aren't enough, there is an even more alarming problem: the political control, mayoral control, of the city's schools. This situation has resulted in business entrepreneurs, nonprofessional educators, running the city schools. Having business leaders run the public schools can be compared to having surgeons working in operating rooms without having gone to medical school. (See Chapter 14, "Deception, Dismantling, and Demise of Public Education," for further discussion of the problems resulting from mayoral control.)

Scarsdale and Great Neck (both in New York) and other similar school districts are run, not by politicians, but by trained professional educators, and their successes are renowned and well documented. In 2009, Scarsdale High School had a graduation rate of 99 percent.[6] For that same year, 98 percent of Great Neck's students also graduated from high school.[7]

The New York City schools and other city schools should look to these successful models to emulate, as should other city schools that are failing to educate all of their students! Unbelievably, other large cities, such as Washington, D.C., are emulating New York City.

I began writing this book in 2006, a year after the publication of Jonathan Kozol's *The Shame of the Nation: The Restoration of Apartheid Schooling in America*.[8] Kozol continues to write about failing city schools and some heroic students; he asks a question I too must ask: Why do city school students have to be heroic in order to be successful? We don't expect superhuman feats from our suburban students. The path is made smooth for them, and no one is surprised when Scarsdale High School sends almost 98 percent of their students to college, many of them to Ivy League schools. That is what is expected of them. They are to become important members of society. Well, city students are no less important. It is time, past time, to fix the city schools and smooth the path—level the playing field—for less wealthy students to achieve whatever they are capable of. That's the American dream that needs to become the American reality. Suburban schools spend double, sometimes triple, the amount of money per student that New York City spends. Across the country, in all the cities, large and small, students are attending segregated and unequal schools. Separate but equal was ruled unconstitutional by the Supreme Court in 1954. What would the highest lawmakers of the land, never mind Martin Luther King Jr. and Rosa Parks, think of what we now have—separate but (grossly) unequal? It is pre-1954 all over again. It is *The Shame of the Nation: The Restoration of Apartheid Schooling in America.*

For students to succeed under these appalling conditions, they must possess a resiliency and superiority that most of us ordinary folk could never muster. What follows next is a chapter about Nobody, me—an ordinary person. It describes how I came to be the teacher I was and what I accomplished during more than three decades of teaching in the Bronx.

2
Nobody

I wrote this book specifically to tell you about my students. My intention was to be the storyteller, not the story. In a world where celebrities rule, fame fades, and idols fall, I am only too glad to have little or no attention focused on me. I am happy to stand outside the crowd and just be myself, my own person. The poet Emily Dickinson said it best:

> I'm nobody! Who are you?
> Are you—nobody—too? . . .
> How dreary—to be—somebody!
> How public. . . .[1]

Without pursuing fame or fortune, I have led a rich and rewarding life.

But we live in a day and age when everybody writes his or her memoir, and maybe, just maybe, a nobody like me should write one too (albeit a short one), just in case there is something in my life that might help you, the reader, with yours. It was never my intention to be different or to do things differently; it just worked out that way.

Certain events and people and ideas molded me into the person I am today. As to which ones had the greatest influence, I couldn't possibly determine. Nonetheless, I'll begin by describing an event that occurred very early in my life, and maybe, just maybe, it was the most profound and influential.

The Little Kidnapper

I don't know the exact date of the kidnapping. I was only about eight at the time. What I do remember is the weather; it was a cold, gray fall day. The few trees on Boynton Avenue, the street in the Bronx where I lived, had lost most of their leaves. I was on my way home after visiting a friend (a play date, in today's parlance). I was in a rush to get home by six o'clock. My father, certainly not a difficult or demanding man, had one rigid household rule: The family—my two brothers, my mother, and I—had to have dinner together every night. (My father was way ahead of his time.) It was a rule we tried hard never to violate.

In my haste to be on time, I almost didn't notice a little three-or four-year-old girl crying. She was sitting on an old milk crate in front of James Monroe High School. I stopped to see what was wrong, and between sobs, she told me that she had been waiting for a long, long time for her father to come out of the school. I looked into the school windows, but there were no lights on, and I couldn't see anything. I walked over to the main entrance to see if any doors were open. The little girl followed me closely and watched as I tried to open each of the five doors. They were all locked, so I took the little girl's outstretched hand and walked to the side entrance, but the doors were locked there too.

It was starting to get dark, and I realized that my parents would be getting worried. I waited just a little while longer, hoping that the blond-haired, blue-eyed girl's father would return. She was shivering, wearing only shorts and a sleeveless blouse. Recalling the novels about Nancy Drew, the detective, I imagined that the little girl had been abandoned by her father because he couldn't afford to feed her.

I knew my parents would feed her and give her a sweater, too (my father was in the sweater business), and so I asked her if she would like to go home with me to get something to eat. She readily agreed (I guess children weren't told to avoid strangers in the late 1940s), and once again, she grabbed my hand and held on tightly. We crossed East 176th Street, looking both ways, as my mother had taught me, and continued walking down Boynton Avenue toward my house. I could see my mother standing on the front stoop, the same stoop used daily for stoop-ball and other games, frantically waving to me. I told you that I was never late. As I approached, I saw my father step outside, too. I explained to them what had happened, and my father said that he would go back to the high school and look for the girl's father.

My mother said that we should go inside to our apartment where she would give the little girl something to eat and a sweater to keep her warm. (I told you she would do that!) By the time she had finished her milk and cookies, my father returned, alone. My parents talked it over and decided that the best thing to do was to call the police. I told my parents that I was afraid that the police would arrest me for kidnapping the little girl. My mother and father assured me that I had done the right thing and that they were very proud of me (music to my ears—then and ever after).

When the officers arrived—two huge, huge uniformed men with shiny badges—they said that they had received a call from a frantic father who reported the kidnapping of his young daughter. (Now I was sure that I was going to jail.) He said that he had left her sitting on a box while he went into Monroe High School to take a test. When he came out, she was gone, and he walked all over looking for her. Finally, he called the police and reported her missing. The extremely tall policemen had smiles on their faces, and one of them bent down and asked me if I were "the little kidnapper." I tried to speak but couldn't, from fear and embarrassment. He said that I had done the right thing: It was right for me to help the little girl, and it was her father who had done the wrong thing. (What a relief that was.) The policemen shook my hand and congratulated me for rescuing the little girl and keeping her safe. Then they left, promising to unite her with her father.

The memory of this incident has stayed with me all these years. I guess it was a turning point, an epiphany, a sudden realization that this was the first time that I really helped someone, and I just knew that it wouldn't be the last.

A Functional Family: Mine

My mother and father had the most everlasting influence on my life, an influence that continues to this very day, twenty-eight years after my mother's death and twenty-four years after my father's death. But before I can begin to tell you about each of them, I have to apologize, most humbly and profusely, for not being able to include them in the more typical dysfunctional family genre. Not only were they extremely "functional"—here's a new category for you—but they were also loving, kind, compassionate, honest, smart people, who were nobodies too, just like me. They never made any headlines or won any awards, but I often thought that if I could bottle their uncommon common sense, their stability, their wisdom, their integrity, their extraordinary people and parenting skills, I could then send the bottles off as my gift to the world to show how to raise a family lovingly and successfully.

My Immigrant Father

My father, a proud American, would never refer to himself as an immigrant, although he was born in Kolomyya, Poland, in 1908 and came to America in 1921. His mother, my grandmother Anna, as a young widow had struggled to support her five children in a very poor, very hostile, anti-Semitic environment. Like many immigrants before her, she dreamed of building a better life for her fatherless family in America. She left some of her children with grandparents and some with other relatives, and, armed mainly with courage (she spoke no English, had few skills and little money), she landed at Ellis Island in 1909. She got a job in a restaurant in the Bronx and eventually met and married a man, who, my father would later say, was one of the finest men he had ever known. Only after their marriage did she tell her new husband that she had left her daughter in Poland and desperately wanted to bring her over to America. He readily consented and paid for my Aunt Fanny, my father's beloved sister, to come here in 1913. My grandmother Anna let some more time pass before she told her husband that she had two sons remaining in Poland and desperately wanted them with her. Once again, this fine gentleman agreed, and thirteen-year-old Irving and sixteen-year-old Herman, my father and uncle respectively, arrived here together in 1921. (World War I had intervened and interfered with immigration.) Jokingly, this remarkable man asked if there were any more children left in Poland and, to his amazement, discovered there were another two. Eventually, he brought them over here, too. If not for this wonderful second husband, all of Anna's five children would have perished along with the two and one-half million other Polish Jews who were murdered during the Holocaust. And I wouldn't be here writing this book today, either.

Although my father was thirteen when he began public school in the Bronx, he was placed in first grade because of the language barrier. By the end of that first year, with nothing but a fierce determination (I inherited that trait) to learn and speak fluent English, with no accent, he was advanced to eighth grade and graduated. This fierce determination would serve him well throughout his life—and mine, too. He had gone to Hebrew School in Poland, the only school where Jews were allowed to get an education, but had not been bar mitzvahed (the bar mitzvah is a Jewish ceremony marking a boy's entrance into manhood). He went by himself to the nearest synagogue in the Bronx and asked the rabbi to perform the ceremony. And so he was bar mitzvahed, without any family present, without any party or any gifts. He did what he had to do, another worthy trait of his that his children would later emulate.

He immediately went to work in a sweater factory, sweeping floors. His mother kept his entire salary, using it to help support the family. Although my father agreed to this arrangement, he told me that whenever he got a raise, he kept the extra money for himself and never told his mother. He was a "shrewdy" all his life, honest and fair but careful to ensure that he wasn't taken advantage of, another admirable trait. Although his formal education ended at the age of thirteen, he was a quick and attentive lifelong learner and one of the smartest men you would ever want to meet. He worked his way up from floor sweeper to sales representative, and only after my older brother and I were out of the house and married did he start his own business. He never made much money; it was not his goal (or my mother's). He was content and happy to be home by six o'clock and have dinner with his family. Family was everything. In the evening, my brothers and I would eagerly await his arrival at the Elder Avenue train station and walk with him up Boynton Avenue, a big hill, to our home. His siblings lived within a few blocks' radius, and we saw our aunts and uncles and cousins all the time. We saw firsthand what a devoted brother, husband, father, and friend he was. When his family or friends needed help, he was always there. He taught me, without preaching, that anyone can stick by you when things were going well, but it was a true test of character to stick by a person when things went badly. Boy, did he score high on that character test.

Being a wonderful parent did not preclude his getting ill. My father had a major heart attack when my older brother and I were young teenagers. He was not able to work for a long time, and we knew we had to help the family. My brother Marty went to work in the neighborhood candy and soda shop after school, weekends, and holidays. At fourteen, I went to work at Lerners' Department Store on 34th Street in Manhattan; I worked every Monday and Thursday night and all day Saturday. We gave half our salary to our father and used the rest to pay for carfare, books, movies, and even the telephone. We worked throughout our high school years. In college, I worked thirty, sometimes forty, hours a week in the Paul Klapper Library. I never got to eat in the college cafeteria or join any clubs or participate in any extracurricular activities. My father did recover eventually and went back to work. But I kept on working, keeping the eighty cents per hour salary I earned (same salary for four years), because earning my own money and helping people in the library contributed not only to my bank account but also to my self-worth and independence. During my fifty-one years of marriage, I have always worked, never wanting my husband to bear the burden of support all by himself.

Mommy Dearest

Describing my mother is going to be risky, especially after I used this well-known disparaging, descriptive term "mommy dearest" for a heading. You are not going to believe what I tell you because so many daughters use those two words sarcastically or ironically; however, I mean the words literally. I can't change my mother's loving and profound influence on me any more than I can change my height or eye color or gene structure. And I wouldn't want to. Martha was the perfect mother for me. (I told you I came from a fully functioning family.) She was smart, practical and idealistic, caring and supportive, and blessed with a good sense of humor. I can still hear her words: "Janet, you need to laugh at yourself more; you take everything too seriously." By the way, I thought that she was beautiful too—a Barbara Stanwyck look-alike, for those readers old enough to remember Barbara Stanwyck, the movie and television star.

My mother was born in the Bronx in 1907, the next-to-youngest of her six siblings. Her mother suffered from high blood pressure, and both her parents died early on. The older brothers and sisters dropped out of school after completing eighth grade in order to support the family. My mother and her younger brother, Louis, were the only ones to graduate from high school. Uncle Lou went on to achieve honors at City College in New York and to graduate from Yale Law School and become a prominent corporate lawyer in Manhattan. His proud brothers and sisters supported him during all his years of schooling, even doing his laundry. Later, when he received fame and fortune (he was a "somebody"), he repaid them all with financial presents but rarely with his actual presence. In 1950, he gave my parents the down payment for our own house. He paid the Rensselaer College tuition for my cousin. (My older brother was offered the same opportunity, but declined it, not wanting to be beholden.) My uncle supported his brothers and sisters financially as they became sick and old. Although he rarely visited (my brothers and I were very critical of him for this failing), my father always defended him by saying that some relatives bother you but never help. Uncle Lou never bothered us, but he always helped. So I have to give him credit for that and thereby place him on my list of major influences.

After graduating from Roosevelt High School in the Bronx, my mother went to work as a bookkeeper and within a few years met and married my father, who was, by now, a sweater salesman. Martha was adored and treasured by my father; anyone and everyone could easily see that. My father was a very humble man and always told me that he couldn't imagine why she had married him, an uneducated, short, stocky foreigner with little potential for financial success. My mother would laugh and say that she knew she would have a good life with him—and so she did! She wasn't seeking money or material things and had very little of both. But she was one of the happiest women you would ever meet.

Martha had three children: My older brother, Marty, was born in 1936, I was born in 1938, and my baby brother, Allan, came along nine years later in 1947. He was born on my parents' fourteenth wedding anniversary, and they would say that he was their best present.

My mother never worked outside of the house; most women didn't in those years. In addition, my father would not have wanted her to work. But his small income meant that his children had few material things: few toys, no books (that's what libraries were for), no music or dance or art lessons, no summer camp (except for a disastrous month spent in a sleep-away charity camp the summer our baby brother was born), and no travel or trips, except to Coney Island in Brooklyn (which we thought was the greatest trip of all). But to tell you the truth, we never felt deprived or poor, mainly because we didn't know many people who had more, and also because my parents were never envious of anyone who did. We were happy to have an at-home mother, and we loved coming home from school at 12:00 for lunch and at 3:00 for milk and cookies and sharing our school day stories with her. We were probably the last in the neighborhood to get a television set, but we did watch the few programs that were on at a friend's house, and that was a lot of fun.

Not having television or computers (not available) or games meant that after school and on weekends and holidays, we played outdoors with neighborhood kids of all ages. There were no arranged playdates like today. We played stoopball, on our own stoop, and handball against the brick wall next door; we jumped rope and engaged in hours and hours of fun playing hide-and-seek and ring-a-lievo. We went bike riding with our used bikes in the nearby schoolyard, and I, in particular, spent endless hours watching the boys play baseball. (My brother would let me play ball only in desperation if no one else showed up.) We played outside in rain, snow, and sleet, and it never cost a penny. In 1948, there was a major snowstorm; schools closed for days, and all the neighborhood kids dug a tunnel from one side of the street to the other and met in the middle. What glorious fun.

My mother washed all our clothes by hand, on a washboard in the bathroom sink. In 1950, we finally got a washing machine, but not a dryer until many years later. She darned all our socks, and to this day, I feel guilty throwing away torn socks. She ironed all our clothes—no permanent press in those years. She tried to teach me, the only daughter (not my brothers), to sew and iron and cook, but I always refused to pay attention; after all, I was going to be a teacher. My mother would laugh, not at my future plans, but at my complete naïveté, because how could I ever get a husband if I lacked these requisite skills? (Remember, these were the 1940s and 1950s, way before women's lib.) At age sixteen, along came Larry, and two days before my twentieth birthday, we were married, without my knowing how to sew, iron, or cook. Goes to show ya!

My mother took great pride in all her children's academic achievements; she fussed over our grades while my father quietly appreciated them. It was assumed that my older brother would go to college. When he came home one day and said that he wanted to open a fruit and vegetable stand, I remember my mother saying that that would be okay, but he would just have to delay his plan until graduation from college, and then, if he still wanted to do that, it would be fine with her. So off he went, to Queens College, with its free tuition, followed by law school at night (no free tuition). Today he is an outstanding accountant and lawyer in New York. Whatever happened to the fruit stand?

But my mother knew that I was the true scholar, the one most interested in learning. My father, however, being old world European, didn't think college was necessary. His argument was that I would get married (wasting my education?), and although Queens College was free, I could be working and contributing to the household, as he had done. Now, my mother was in no way a weak personality, but she did save her assertiveness for only the biggest battles, for what she fiercely believed was right, and she fiercely believed that I should go to college and become a teacher. So, my mother threatened to go out and get a job, if need be, so that I could continue my education and follow my dream. I've told you that my father didn't want my mother to work outside the home, ever, but my mother usually got her way when she threatened to get a job. And so she did get her way. I think he knew from the beginning that this battle was one he couldn't win. Can you imagine what would have happened to me if I hadn't become a teacher? I might have had to learn to sew and cook and iron.

There are some people who grow up wishing they had better or different parents. But my brothers and I grew up knowing that we had the best mom and dad. Cousins and friends, who often congregated in our house, would tell us repeatedly that they loved visiting us because it was such a happy household. And so it was.

In 1982, my mother died suddenly, from a heart attack. Four years later, my father died, also from a heart attack, while watching his favorite baseball team, the Mets, lose another game. His funeral was delayed, allowing time for Larry and me to fly home from Copenhagen. My brothers and I sat shiva, a period of mourning in the Jewish religion, during which, after burial, friends and family visit and console and reminisce. As my brothers and I relived old memories, my older brother decided that it was time to confess. He wanted the truth told: He was the favorite child. My younger brother, with a big grin on his face, contradicted Marty and said, "You got it all wrong, big brother. I, the baby of the family, was definitely the favorite." At this point, I could hardly restrain myself because, as the only daughter, I knew, without a doubt, that I was truly the favorite. We three looked at each other, let the revelations sink in, and then we laughed and laughed. Yes, the truth had finally been revealed. We were all three of us the favorites. Our parents had managed (don't ask me how, I told you that I wanted to bottle their parenting skills) to make their three children feel so important, so special, so valued, that each one was convinced that he or she was the favored one. The rabbi who visited us during our mourning period said that he had never heard children talk so glowingly of their parents. What a legacy they left us. They were the best of parents—and we always knew it.

My Older Brother

Marty's job, from the age of three, was to watch out for me. Growing up, I was thrilled that he allowed me to play with him; I was so glad to join in his fun and games, even if I were only filling in for an absent player. He took me every Saturday afternoon to the Ward Movie Theater on Westchester Avenue. It cost twelve cents for the ticket and five cents for the candy bar, and for a total of seventeen cents we would sit there all afternoon watching two full-length movies, ten cartoons, one serial cliffhanger (to be continued the following week), and the news of the week (no television news at that time). As a result of these Saturday excursions, I became a lifelong lover of the movies. (Dating Larry, I would convince him to sometimes see three films in one day at three different theaters, a practice he abandoned, to my dismay, soon after we married. "Two a day are enough," he would say. He definitely married me under false pretenses.)

My brother took his responsibilities seriously, and as I grew into my teenage years, he always questioned me: "Where are you going? With whom?" He once reported to my mother that I had been seen "holding hands" with Larry on the Queens College campus. (I guess I just had to marry Larry after that indiscretion.) My mother said that Marty had gotten carried away and explained to me that long after she was gone, he would always be my big brother and my protector. As the years have passed, my mother's words have come true, and no sister ever had a better bigger brother. (How could I not look up to him when on a prominent shelf in his law office sits a copy of one of my all-time favorite books, John F. Kennedy's *Profiles in Courage,* biographies of famous politicians who had the courage of their convictions.)

My Baby Brother, "Precious"

Allan was nine years younger than I, and I called him "precious" until he was seventeen, when he asked me to stop using that word in front of his friends (but I could continue doing so in private). My mother gave me enormous responsibilities in helping raise him, and I mothered him all his life. I took him to his first day of kindergarten, first day of high school, and, believe it or not, his first day of college. When Larry and I were dating and even after we married, we took him with us wherever we went.

Caring for my little brother was a natural stepping-stone in the development of my character and my lifelong drive to help people. He was in the seventh grade when I began teaching at his junior high school. He and his friends would go out of their way to pass my classrooms and yell, "Hi, Janet"—an unheard-of breach of propriety. With my help, I like to think, Allan grew up successfully, married his high school sweetheart, became a tax accountant, and raised two fine sons. But, he is—was—and always will be—"precious."

My Husband—Cutest Feller I Ever Saw

There is no doubt that the most powerful, loving, all-embracing influence in my life has been my husband of almost fifty-one years, Larry. He was the cutest feller I ever saw. I met him when I was sixteen, and, as I always told my students, he still is the cutest feller I ever saw. We got married before I was twenty, and relatives and friends would say to my mother, "How could you let her get married at such a young age?" My mother's reply: "Not to worry; they will overcome that problem soon enough." And so we did.

The year of our marriage, 1958, Larry was to have graduated from Rensselaer Polytechnic Institute with a degree in electrical engineering. But the year before, in 1957, he changed colleges and careers, to my complete happiness. He enrolled at New York University (NYU) in Manhattan, majored in biology, took the New York City teachers' exam, got the highest score, and became an outstanding New York City high school biology teacher. Every student in his class wanted to become either a biologist or a scientist or a doctor. (I know that because we taught in the same high school.) His career change meant everything to me because now I was able to share this vital part of my life with the most important person in my life.

In the 1960s, he completed his master's degree and all the course work for his doctorate at NYU. A college credit cost $25 then, and it took almost all our money to pay the tuition. A teacher's salary was $4,800 a year at that time and remained at that level for years. A new library was built at NYU during the years Larry attended, and, to this day, whenever we pass by, we tell everyone that we built that library.

My husband received the finest training in the art and science of teaching at NYU's School of Education. Our U.S. secretary of education, Arne Duncan, appointed by President Barack Obama, calls teaching an art, not a science, but he is very wrong! Teaching is a science, based on scientific research, both theoretical and practical. The art, as in any profession, is based on knowing how to implement the sound, well-tested research, the backbone of any professional endeavor. In an article titled "Taking Educational Research to School," Mark Seidenberg of the department of psychology, University of Wisconsin, writes, "Enormous progress has been made in understanding the behavioral and neuro-biological bases of learning. . . . What is remarkable is how little of this research has penetrated educational practice. Teachers are not exposed to this research as part of their training. I often speak with teachers who are surprised that a science of reading exists, not to mention a science of learning."[2] Shouldn't Mr. Duncan know about the art and science of teaching? Our secretary of education has an impressive biography, having served on many boards of education and foundations. He was super-intendent of Chicago schools. *But, he was never a teacher.*[3] In chapter 14

I provide more information about how essential it is for every school administrator to have had experience as a teacher.

The education courses that my husband took at NYU helped make him and me master teachers. My education courses at Queens College were inadequate, taught by professors who had never worked with large-sized classes in large cities. NYU professors were on the firing line, working in the city schools, and the expertise Larry gained from them, he shared with me. He became my role model and mentor for my entire professional life and private life, too. After working as a master science teacher for ten years, he became the assistant principal in charge of science, formerly called chairman of the science department, in a new Bronx high school. There, he trained many young men and women to be outstanding science educators. After ten award-winning years as an assistant principal, he left to become a high school principal of renown. As principal, he was able to combine and use all his talents: master teacher, master teacher of teachers, an inquiring mind, great intellect, knowledge and love of music and art and literature, great leadership skills, and people skills, along with compassion and understanding of what it means to be human and humane. I measure all principals by his outstanding qualities, and I look around and see few of his caliber. It makes me so sad to see how low the bar has been set for new principals. Many have hardly taught but are armed with business degrees and given training in a business model that may work well in a factory or office, but not in a school. The principals, as the title implies, should be the principal teachers. Are they? Maybe someday, my husband and others like him could be cloned.

My Loving Sons

Growing up, as I have told you, I had only one goal—to be a teacher. Marrying and having babies, the dream of many girls of my generation and earlier ones, was not for me. That is, until I met Larry and included him in my future plans. At twenty-two, I had my first son, Stuart, and at twenty-five, I had my second son, Jeffrey. How young and ingenuous I was to have thought at one time that babies were not for me. Not only did my sons thoroughly enrich my life, but they taught me what it means to be fully human, to be responsible for a living person's every breath and well-being. I learned from them what it means to be tolerant and patient, flexible and compassionate, giving and loving and empathetic, too. I may not have been as successful at parenting as my parents were, but it sure wasn't because I didn't try. When my older son went off to college, he told us that he felt that he had grown up with us, and so he did. Becoming mature, having my sons, made me not only a better person, but a more complete fully functioning one.

I wanted passionately for my sons to love learning and to be happy in school. And what I wanted for my sons, I wanted for my students. For forty-two years, come every September, I would welcome every new class and tell them that what I wanted for them was exactly what I wanted for my own two children. Half of my students would believe me right away, but I would have to earn the trust of the others, and I promised them that I would. I strived to get the right balance both for my sons and my students; however, although I could control the atmosphere for learning in my own classes, I could not control it in my sons'. As a result, more often than not, they were unhappy in school and truly believed that learning began after three o'clock, when they got home. As for my students, you would have to ask them if they were happy and learning in my class.

All I know is that having my own children made me appreciate and love every student, boy or girl, who walked into my classroom. Having sons made me learn about and understand better the needs and problems and concerns of young people. Having sons made me a better human being. I judge the quality of any school by the same standards I used to judge my sons' schools: Was the New York City school in which I was teaching good enough for my sons? If not, how could I help to make it better?

Nobody: That's Me!

In high school, I was a very good student, doing well in almost all of my classes except for physical education, my bête noire. The English classes were definitely my favorites. When I got to college and majored in English, I was amazed that I was given college credit for reading books that I always wanted to read, the so-called world's greatest literature. I did notice that the curriculum centered on dead white male writers and an occasional dead white female writer. After graduation, I would discover more contemporary writers, male and female, alive and well, from diverse cultures; eventually I would include them in a new curriculum for a multicultural literature course that became my specialty. For now, I want to tell you about a social studies class that had a tremendous empowering influence on me.

College Knowledge

A two-year course in contemporary civilization was mandated for every Queens College student in the 1950s. One of these classes in particular stands out vividly in my mind. An event occurred there that probably altered the course my life would take. We were assigned to read about a murder case that had been brought to trial some years earlier. We were to read all the court documents and come to class prepared to act as a jury and decide the fate of the accused man. Only the professor knew the outcome, and he promised to tell us at the end whether we had reached the same decision as the real jury. I remember sitting in a circle and listening to arguments by other students. Many of them agreed almost immediately that the accused was guilty. Only three of us thought otherwise. After a few more discussions over a few days, everyone in the class, except me, was convinced of the man's guilt. Some students were annoyed at me for not agreeing with them and for prolonging the discussion. I tried to present my ideas carefully and deliberately, going home at night and rereading all the documents (after 11:00 P.M., of course, when I got home from my library job and had done all my other homework). I was persistent because I believed that the accused was really innocent, based on the facts of the case. I wouldn't be intimidated into changing my mind, not even when a fellow student said, under his breath, that I was stupid and stubborn. I never did give in, and finally, the professor called a halt to any further discussion. And then he told us the true outcome: The jury had found the man innocent. I was right, and the class and the professor applauded me loudly. He said that he had tried this same case in his other class, and there the guilty decision had been unanimous. From this experience, I learned to stick to my guns when I thought I was right, even if what I thought differed from everyone else's point of view. Not only was I proud of myself, but the lesson of speaking out and being true to myself and my beliefs, and being willing to suffer the consequences if my choice of action didn't work out, would influence me greatly throughout my life, especially, as you will see, regarding a school incident that I will tell you about shortly.

More College Influences—Books and More Books

As a young person growing up in a lower socioeconomic class (not that I knew that's what it would be called), I hadn't gone anywhere beyond the metropolitan area, meaning New York and New Jersey. It was through books that I traveled, not only around the world, but to other times in history also. (As Emily Dickinson wrote, "There is no frigate like a book,"[4] which is reprinted in note 4.) I became a world traveler without ever traveling.

In my fourth-year Spanish class in college, I had to read, in the original Spanish, Cervantes' *Don Quixote*, quite a linguistic challenge for me. To use a more popular phrase of today, I was "blown away" by this unforgettable character who tilted at windmills, saw a prostitute as his lady and an old sidekick as a dashing hero, and, in general, saw life through rose-colored glasses. As so many have through the centuries, I identified with Don Quixote's optimistic, idealistic, and impractical outlook. Regardless of the cynicism around me (cynicism that is even more prominent today), I have an abiding faith in people and a profound belief that the world can be made better, and we can all play our part in improving it. I also realize that my eternal optimism annoys some people, but I also know that I couldn't and wouldn't change my nature. Let others change theirs!

Since I worked throughout high school and college, time has always pressed in on me, forcing me to allocate it carefully. I made up my mind, early on, to read the best books by the best writers and not waste time on what I call frivolous reading, such as mysteries (sorry, Mr. King, Mr. Patterson, etc.), chick lit, and best sellers of dubious distinction. Rather, I would concentrate on reading past and present books by Nobel Prize winners, Pulitzer Prize winners, National Book Award winners, Man Booker Prize winners, and all other award-winning authors from around the world. In this way, and to this day, I can keep up with what the greatest minds are thinking and writing about. My reading list includes both fiction and nonfiction on a fairly equal basis.

But—the two books that changed me the most were brought home by my husband from New York University. You probably never heard of these books, but nevertheless, they exerted a major and profound influence on my professional life and helped me put into action what I always believed in my heart and mind to be true.

On my desk at home sits a plaque given to me in 2002 at my retirement from full-time teaching in the Bronx (since then I have been teaching part-time). It reads thus: "Presented to a Master Teacher and shining example of 'Teaching as a Subversive Activity' in honor of forty-two years of dedication to the children of New York City." So there it is, a reference to the book that influenced me deeply and unalterably. Although this book, *Teaching as a Subversive Activity,* was written in 1969, it should be required reading today for every citizen, parent, teacher, administrator—even mayor! It is the thesis of this book that "change—constant, accelerating, ubiquitous—is the most striking characteristic of the world we live in and that our educational system has not yet recognized this fact."[5] The authors, Neil Postman and Charles Weingartner, made that statement forty years ago, and it is even more relevant today as we witness the rapid pace of change in our society. The authors also wrote that "the schools do little or nothing to encourage youth to question, doubt or challenge any part of the society in which they live."[6] (Standardized testing does not test for these purposes, obviously.)

I need to tell you about one of the best lessons I ever saw, which will better illustrate what Postman and Weingartner are talking about. This lesson occurred in a Problems in American Democracy class. At the beginning of the term, students, many living in the Bronx projects or other low-income housing, were asked to describe, in both written and pictorial form, the problems they faced in their homes, their buildings, their streets, and their community. Together with their excellent social studies teacher, who facilitated the project, they explored and learned all about the resources, agencies, politicians, and community organizers who could help them deal with such problems as their lack of heat and electricity, their broken plumbing, the filthy and decaying halls, rats, guns, drugs on the street, and more. After gathering all the information, they wrote letters and made phone calls to the people who could help; they organized other tenants; they showed up at officials' offices and meetings and in general, did everything they could to solve their very real-life problems. I was privileged to see the finished projects at the end of the term. Each student had completed a portfolio, which included all correspondence, dates, and times of meetings, and, best of all, there were "before and after" pictures taken so that the students' accomplishments could be easily seen.

This was "authentic" education, what schools should really be about. This very fine teacher empowered his students, changed not only their behavior but their lives. (That's as good a definition of education or learning that you'll ever see: Learning is a change in behavior.) The only behavior that changes after studying for standardized tests is negative: Students who may have liked school and learning now may come to hate it. Very little of what is relevant to life is taught in schools. In the city schools, so many students enter with weak skills and are in need of more and more drill to pass these tests, and so less and less time is spent in art, music, science, drama, dance, orchestra, and even gym and recess.

In the end, whether they drop out or graduate, they have added nothing to the advancement of knowledge, the enjoyment of their lives, their employment, or solving the world's problems. The politicians and business people (and educators who should know better, but don't) believe that what can't be graded isn't important. (How can you measure appreciation and love of music, art, dance, literature, creativity, and talent?) The leaders have lost their way and fail to focus on the essence of education. As Postman and Weingartner say, "The so-called high standards really represent the lowest possible standards imaginable. There should be new standards for learning as distinct from standards for grading. The human condition can be improved through education."[7] This idea is well illustrated in the course I described above. No Child Left Behind, along with its main feature, standardized testing, and Race to the Top, the newest educational reform program, do nothing to improve the human condition. At the very least, these similar programs should be examined and fundamentally changed.

If you are interested in reading more about Postman and Weingartner's ideas, see quotes from their book in note 8.[8] You won't be disappointed!

The other book that really shook me up was *The Saber-tooth Curriculum*, by J. Abner Peddiwell (a pseudonym of Harold Raymond Wayne Benjamin). It was written in 1939! It is as pertinent today as it was then—maybe even more so! A quick summary will suffice to show you why it had such a strong influence on me. The book is set in a mythical land where life is centered on fish grabbing, horse clubbing, and tiger scaring. Learning to perform these tasks was the essence and goal of education because the results led to a better life for all. Food, shelter, clothing, and security were provided for the entire tribe. None were left out (unlike today's society). However, times changed: The fish, the horses, and the tigers eventually disappeared, but the schools went on teaching fish grabbing, horse clubbing, and tiger scaring. The so-called wise men of the community, the leaders, refused to change the curriculum despite devastating conditions; they adhered to the belief that "the essence of true education is timelessness. You must know that there are some eternal verities and the saber-tooth curriculum is one of them."[9] What began as purposeful education degenerated into useless education.

Now, we know that there are no eternal verities; all we can count on is that things will change. Our educational system desperately needs to update its curriculum to reflect the changing times. If you are interested in learning more about what J. Abner Peddiwell had to say, please read his book; it is replete with powerful ideas.

In the 1980s, there was an academic feud raging on campuses and schools everywhere between multiculturists and traditionalists; traditionalists favored the old classics, and multiculturists wanted to introduce more diversity, allowing for the changing times as well as the changing population. Now, granted, I wasn't a curriculum specialist or an administrator. I was nobody, but as a teacher of English, I saw firsthand that many students, instead of being turned on to books, were turned off by works that no longer spoke to them or dealt with their own lives, problems, or interests. There was no doubt that many students had very weak reading skills, but I was convinced that if they were given more exciting, contemporary works to read, along with receiving help in improving their reading skills, students could develop a lifelong love of reading. Later on, after getting students hooked on books, they could be introduced to the classics. Many students told me how they hated reading (how painful to hear that), and when asked to name one book they had liked, a ninth-grade youngster, with a second-grade reading level, confessed that the best book she had ever read was *The Happy Hooker*. (An adult book, don't you think?) How did she manage to read that book? An inaccurate reading score? Very possible. Strong motivation to understand the story? Very possible. Attempting to teach Shakespeare, Wordsworth, Keats, Byron, or even Dickens often became an exercise in futility. Oh, teachers said they "taught" these authors' works, but I knew that students never really understood these authors. I realized that I had to learn how to improve teenagers' reading skills, not for standardized tests, which, mercifully, were nonexistent in the 1960s, 1970s, and 1980s, but so that my students could read books that could change their lives, as books had changed mine.

I went back to college in the 1970s, at night, teaching full-time during the day and balancing (or not) my life as a wife and mother of two young sons. I received my master's degree in reading and felt fully armed to help my students.

I have told you that I sought out and read multicultural literature for my own edification and enjoyment. Often, I would select excerpts from my readings and share them with my regular English classes. Once, I brought in an excerpt from Julia Alvarez's book, *How the Garcia Girls Lost Their Accents*, a semiautobiographical account of Julia and her three sisters' adjustment to life in the Bronx after migrating from the Dominican Republic. My students loved the excerpt: Not only did they want to read the entire book, but they also wanted to know if I could bring in books by Puerto Rican writers, too. So I introduced them to Rosario Ferré, a writer alive and well in Puerto Rico, as well as Esmeralda Santiago and her book, *When I Was Puerto Rican*. In 1987, August Wilson, the soon-to-be esteemed black playwright, won the Pulitzer Prize for his play *Fences*. With the help of my very supportive English chairwoman, I was able to obtain copies of this play for my students. When I told my classes that August Wilson was a high school dropout who had overcome many obstacles on the road to success, they were eager, yes, eager, to read the play.

It was this experience of teaching *Fences* that gave me the impetus to try to create a multicultural literature course. I had to make a presentation to the entire English department to state my case as to why this literature was not only important, but extremely worthwhile, too. I prepared for this presentation carefully and methodically, knowing that there were some teachers who were either against this new course or not knowledgeable themselves about the explosion and publication of prolific writers of all ethnicities and cultures. (August Wilson would go on to write ten plays and win the Pulitzer Prize, twice.)

By the time I finished my presentation trying to convince the entire English department that multicultural literature was challenging, amazing, and award-winning, and that students could be turned on (as they were) to literature that spoke to their needs, interests, and problems, and that these writers were reporting on the human condition, regardless of their nationality, the die was cast, and the entire department accepted the new curriculum that I knew better reflected our changing society. (It also helped that I gave new book talks every term on staff development day.)

Convincing my colleagues was the first challenge; the second was my concern that my black and Hispanic students might not readily accept a little middle-aged Jewish woman as an expert in black and Hispanic literature. Would a minority teacher do a better job or be a better fit? Since there wasn't a minority teacher who could or would teach this new course, by default, I got the job. I did voice my concern to a young Hispanic social studies teacher (who, by the way, rode his bicycle to school every day from New Jersey), and who convinced me that this little middle-aged Jewish lady would be the right person because of the breaking of barriers and the buildup of trust I had already achieved. I hoped that—maybe—he was right.

The course became very popular. You make think I lack all humility, but I am very proud of turning kids on to great literature. (If you would like to see some of my students' comments, see letters on pages 34 and 35.) Originally, the course was open to eleventh and twelfth graders who had already passed the English regents and could afford to "waste"(?) their time. But as word spread, other students who were eager to read about multicultural writers enrolled. Depending on who signed up for my course, and for how many terms, I changed the curriculum. One term, I had a beautiful Arab girl in my class, and that term and thereafter, I included the Egyptian writer, Naguib Mahfouz, the winner of the Nobel Prize for Literature in 1988. Some students were part Native American, and so Michael Dorris and Louise Erdrich got included, permanently. A few Chinese students enrolled, and that's how the Chinese American writer Amy Tan joined us. And so on. Whatever the literature, I emphasized our common humanity and, in essence, how alike we are. All students, regardless of their background, were exposed to multicultural writers. (Votes for best book were overwhelmingly for *Love in the Time of Cholera* by Gabriel García Márquez, the Colombian writer who won the Nobel Prize for literature in 1982; votes for best poet were for Pablo Neruda, the Latin American poet who won the Nobel Prize for literature in 1971; and votes for best book by a black writer were for *The Bluest Eye*, written by Nobel Prize–winner Toni Morrison.) See Appendix B for the entire Course of Study for Multicultural Literature.

A television reporter, Pablo Guzman, came to Carter High School to interview my class and me regarding our feelings about this new course. It is hard to believe all this happened only twenty-five years ago. We appeared on the six o'clock news that day. In addition to that fame, Mercy College, a four-year Westchester college with branches in the Bronx, offered three college credits to students who successfully completed my course. I had to submit my credentials and a copy of the curriculum for their faculty approval. I also had to appear for an interview. All these tasks were completed favorably. Mercy College professors frequently observed my classes, and shortly after, they offered free four-year college scholarships to Carter High School Students who maintained an overall 85 average. I like to think that this extremely generous gift was given because of the college's favorable introduction to my students in the multicultural literature class.

Literature had changed my world (and continues to do so), and from feedback from my students, their world was changed too. Some of my students went off to college and majored in multicultural literature; they would write to me and suggest books that I might like to read. What a joy. My students became my teachers. Some went on to become teachers themselves. Others became lifelong readers, and I know this because they continue to write to me. One young man who had planned to be a funeral director changed his goals after being in my class and went on to become a teacher—like me, he said. A few years later, he regretted to inform me that teaching was not for him and he was going back to enroll in mortuary school. He was a wonderful young man, and I'm sure he found success in his chosen field.

I know that it is obvious to you that I loved teaching; however, what you don't know is that I almost gave it up. Read on.

A New Teacher: Trials and Tribulations

Even with my fierce determination to be a teacher, the first day and the first year of teaching almost did me in. So if you happen to be beginning a new career, teaching or otherwise, the next part may be of help to you.

I graduated from Queens College in January 1960 and began teaching soon after in a middle-class junior high school. My kid brother was in seventh grade at that very school. My college supervisor had highly recommended me for the position. The principal's interview went well, and I was excited to begin my long-awaited career. But, after my first day's devastating experience, it amazes me that I ever went back. I got to school so early (always a plus) that I had to wait for the building to open and get my teaching program and keys. The principal came late, handed me my program and keys, and offered these words of encouragement: "Good luck—you're going to need it." I had hoped that he would show me where my classrooms (all five of them) were located, but he quickly disappeared. Finding my first classroom, with the help of my brother's friends, took longer than I thought, and as soon as I entered the room, students stampeded in, pushing and shoving and yelling and eager to see the new teacher—me. I tried to quiet them down and introduce myself at the same time. Some asked if I were really Allan's sister and applauded and whistled when I confirmed that I was. The room was packed with students, and boys and girls were fighting over the too few seats. Many sat on the windowsill, and when I finally quieted them down and took their attendance, I counted forty-nine. They told me one boy was absent; there were really fifty in the class. All of them wanted to tell me what they had endured since September; I said that I would listen to them— one at a time. I learned that there had been a succession of substitutes, and most had been driven out by the students' poor behavior. Although panic crept through my body, I tried to appear cool, calm, and collected. I assured them that I was here to stay and that I would do my best to help them catch up on missed work.

The first order of business was to get about ten kids off the windowsill. I put two at my desk, two on the desk, and asked the others to please sit on the floor in front of the room where they could see and hear me. At the very least, I felt I saved kids from falling out the windows, since there were no screens. To my amazement, they listened to me, and I promised to rotate them around the room until I could find more seats. I then asked them to take out their books so that I could see what they were using. They all laughed and said that they had no books—no English books or history books. Were they teasing me? I didn't think so because I would have expected at least one student to respond correctly, and not one did. I told them that although I felt bad about their lack of history books, my concern was more for the lack of English books. It was then that some students told me that they needed both books in this core class, a double period of English and social studies combined. The principal, in his haste, had neglected to tell me that I had two classes, double periods, of so-called core, in four different rooms.

The fifth classroom, I discovered, was an art room—my art room— and I would teach art there every day, five days a week, for the rest of the school year. That first art class was a disaster, as I feared, but falling back on my inner art resources, I gave it a try. My key unlocked the closet, and, lo and behold, there were supplies. I gave them out, and to my shock, the students threw everything, crayons, clay, even paint, all over the room. The art class had fifty students also, and some were in my core class and tried to help me. I learned, after this day, *never* to give out art supplies and to allow students to use only their own pencils and papers. Well, I had no curriculum and no books, and I was teaching art and history out of license (in high school each subject area had its own license, and I had only an English license) to students who had gone wild because of so many substitutes.

My first day was not what I had expected, to put it mildly. At three o'clock, after bus duty, another job I didn't know anything about, I had stomach cramps and a blinding headache—maladies I had rarely suffered. I decided to go see my mother for consolation, and I cried all the way there. My mother told me that day two would be better. Later, when my husband came home, I told him that I wanted to quit—even though I had wanted to be a teacher since I was five years old. He reminded me that we had just moved into our own apartment, having lived with my parents up to then. Also, he was still in college, and our tuition bills were mounting. He gave me aspirin and assured me that my next day would be better. If I had been born rich, I probably would have quit then and there.

I did go back, with a fierce determination to tackle all the problems, one at a time, and give teaching another try. I obtained a curriculum guide from another teacher (the principal had none left) and found old books hidden in a closet. Once again, I used inner resources I didn't know I had, and I began to organize my classes and my students. I literally begged the custodian to find more chairs for my rooms, and, miraculously, he did. I think my students felt sorry for me, because I was young and because I was Allan's sister, and, to my amazement, they cooperated. After the first week, the principal came in to observe me and congratulated me on having all my students seated and all the window shades at uniform level, mighty important accomplishments in junior high. He never appeared again, nor did any other administrator. So much for staff development for new teachers. It didn't exist in those years. (It was later initiated by the emerging teachers' union's push for professionalism.)

The Union

Word circulated, after I had been there for a few weeks, that an after-school meeting was being called by a group of teachers who were hoping to join a citywide movement to form a teachers' union. The aim was to help improve working conditions, salaries, and student achievement. The administration voiced concern that it was unprofessional to belong to a union. (Unions, in 1960, existed mainly for blue-collar workers.) Instinctively, I knew that I had to help make things better, and, together with other teachers (in unity there is strength), I went to the first meetings of what would become the United Federation of Teachers. We were asked to write about our concerns, in order of priority, followed by a discussion of the issues. To my amazement, mainly because I didn't think it was proper, not that it wasn't vital, the top of the list was dirty bathrooms and lack of soap and toilet paper. At my very last union meeting, forty-two years later, lack of these basic necessities still topped the list. (See next chapter for more details.)

Items on the agenda included teaching out of license (a chronic problem to this day); no preparation periods; uncapped class size; covering classes instead of duty-free lunch periods (I hadn't had a free lunch period

yet); a dress code that forced women to wear skirts, not pants; no grievance procedure; mandatory leave for pregnant women; and, among other
issues, no input into any school matter, professional or otherwise. How
could I not become an active union member when I believed in all the
issues being fought over? I had no idea, as a new teacher, that there were
problems that needed to be addressed in the school system. I thought
and hoped that I could make changes in my own classroom, but I never
expected to be part of a big organization that would help make teaching
truly a profession. Al Shanker, the first UFT president, became an elo-
quent spokesperson for all city teachers, and under his inspired leadership, enormous positive changes were made, and teachers finally were
treated professionally, although it took a number of citywide strikes to
make these changes. (Someday I would like to write a book about conditions in the city schools before and after unionization.) I went on to
become an active member of the UFT executive board in both high
schools where I worked, eventually winning the highest union honor,
the Trachtenberg Award, for revitalization of an inactive union as well as
for strong union leadership. That story is coming up next!

My Day in Court

In the 1980s, I was deeply involved, along with a few other brave colleagues, in bringing charges against an unfit principal who was abusive
to staff and students. It's a long story, and there are many people out
there who were victims of this principal's abuse and vindictiveness. After
sitting back and observing, for three years, the harm that this administrator was inflicting on others (he had thought highly of me, even recom-
mending me for the Best Teacher Award), I helped (how I hate injustice)
to organize a concerted effort to have this principal removed. I rallied
the troops, so to say, by quoting the eighteenth-century writer Edmund
Burke: "The only thing necessary for the triumph of evil is for good
men to do nothing." And we were good men and women.

I helped assemble huge dossiers, not an easy task because so many
teachers and administrators were afraid to speak up; some couldn't
because they themselves would be implicated in the abusive practices.
Union meetings had to be held out of school because this principal disal-
lowed them, illegal under hard-fought union regulations. The few times
we were able to meet on school property, the small number of teachers
who attended and weren't intimidated were called into his office the

next day and questioned about the attendees and the discussions, guaranteeing poor attendance or none at future meetings. The union helped arrange a meeting with the new superintendent of New York City schools in June, and two other teachers and I presented our three-hundred-page document to this wonderful lady. She was very attentive and promised to read the entire dossier over the summer and get back to us in the fall. We were quite elated by her response and were sure that proper action would be taken.

But—there is always a "but"—this superintendent was removed from office in August, and we had to begin all over again. The abusive practices continued, and finally, with the help of a very fine young UFT lawyer, we were able to bring a case before the New York Labor Relations Board (NYLRB) citing antilabor law violations. (To me, it was like catching murderers on tax fraud when all else failed.) I testified in court, as did several other colleagues, and we won the case.

But, but, but . . . the NYLRB, while finding this man guilty, did not have the power to either remove him from office or impose any kind of sentence. It was up to the board of education to take action, and in their wisdom (?), they decided only to monitor his actions for the next three years. I don't know if they did it or not, because I did not continue working there. I could not look at myself in the mirror if I had remained. So, although I loved this school and its students (hundreds and hundreds of them signed a petition to the principal, within a few hours of learning about my transfer, pleading with him to disallow the transfer I had requested), I decided to leave. And so I did. At the end of three years, the so-called monitor was removed, and this principal went on wreaking havoc over his staff and students. Did I feel bad that I lost this battle? Yes, I certainly did, but I felt some measure of satisfaction in having tried to make things better. A very dear friend and colleague, a renowned social studies teacher who left when I did, reminded me that nobody ever got Hitler, but it sure was vital to try.

Maybe there is a somewhat happy ending to this story after all. After twenty-five years, terrible that it took so long, this principal was finally forced to resign or face charges. He chose resignation, and although justice was delayed for so long, it was, at long last, not denied.

I'm happy. I'm nobody. I am my own person. I will go on trying to make things better, knowing that there are other people out there, nobodies like me, who are trying to do the same. The next chapter is an excruciatingly painful physical description of my school, written so that you will know what the school conditions were like for my students, before you meet them in Part II.

To
Mrs. Nayer

You are a very special person. I know this for a fact because your kind heart shines through every day. I want to thank you for the profession you have choosen. You capture the essence of teaching. You have the wonderful ability to make your student feel good about themselves. A pride in oneself that only comes when takes the time to care and that's exactly what you do. It has been a great honor for me to have been a student in your class.

Love always,
Heather

To:
  Mrs. Mayer,

As I have said before, if I spent a lifetime trying to repay you for what you have given me, I would die a man in debt. Thank you so very much.

Booker T. Washington was indeed right when he said, "There is no education which consist of books and costly apparatus that is equal to coming in contact with great individuals. I have had the pleasure of coming in contact with a great individual, and that is you! Your knowledge will be with me always.

Love
Mel

3

It Was the Worst of Times

In 1975, America was in the midst of yet another economic crisis, and New York City was close to financial ruin.[1] Mayor Abraham Beame and Governor Hugh Carey looked to President Gerald Ford for a bailout, and on August 30, 1975, the *New York Daily News* printed as its headline what was essentially Ford's response: "DROP DEAD."[2] (His callous response was in stark contrast to President Barack Obama's response to the financial crisis, in 2009, of giving federal bailouts to major financial institutions, auto companies, and insurance giants.)

Mayor Beame, on the eve of filing for bankruptcy, successfully negotiated an agreement with Albert Shanker, president of the United Federation of Teachers, later to become president of the American Federation of Teachers. City officials said that they had no other sources of cash in reserve and that the teachers' union was all that separated them from declaring bankruptcy. Mr. Shanker agreed to commit $150 million, a huge sum in 1975, of teacher pension money to bail out the city. Even with the teachers' largess, thousands of teachers were let go, take-home pay was cut, and wages were frozen at the pre-June 1975 level.[3]

It was at this time that repairs to public schools ended abruptly—with catastrophic results, as you shall see.

In 1985, ten years after New York City's financial distress, I transferred from the (mostly) all-white Harriman High School in the Bronx, to the (mostly) all black and Hispanic Carter High School in the Bronx, a distance of only a few miles, but in terms of the physical plant and student population, worlds apart. Harriman High School was just thirteen years old, and hadn't yet reached its prime. Carter High School, at sixty-two years of age, was way past its prime. Was it significant that in 1985, thirty-one years after the Supreme Court's ruling that "separate but equal" was anything but, we were back where we started?

It was apparent immediately, as soon as I entered Carter, that it was a decaying infrastructure. Unfortunately, there were so many more schools just like it.[4] I didn't know then that this building would be grossly neglected for another fifteen years, almost until the year 2000.

For a total of twenty-five years, 1975–2000, an entire generation of students would pass through this crumbling school, damaging not only their health and physical safety but also their self-esteem. It is important, for you, the reader, to understand the overwhelming obstacles many Bronx students faced not only in their homes and streets but also in their schools. As you read further in my book and come to understand what my students endured, you will be better able to judge if Bronx high school students are really "as bad as they say."

The best way that I can describe the physical conditions of Carter and make you "see" how it functioned—or didn't—is to take you with me through a typical day in my life as a Bronx high school teacher, and let you see, in a compressed or snapshot form, all the problems for yourself. Now, not all the incidents occurred every day, but they did occur often enough to enable you to get the picture. Nothing is exaggerated—every teacher can corroborate what I am about to tell you—so be prepared!

Come—walk with me.

It is a Monday morning in October, 7:30 A.M., and I am just arriving at Carter High School. It is a scramble to find a parking spot in this very old, but fairly well preserved Italian neighborhood, just a few blocks from Fordham University, the Bronx Zoo, and the Botanical Gardens. These three sites will be vastly improved over the years, unlike the public schools. Priorities, I guess. There are many two-story houses mixed in with apartment houses sharing the street with Carter, so parking anywhere in the neighborhood is extremely difficult. Arriving early enables me to park in the fenced-in schoolyard, formerly a playground. This playground is a reminder that this school began its life in 1923 as an elementary school, and remnants of its early days still remain. (When we enter the building, notice the very narrow, dark halls, built for small children and small adults? Also, you'll see two sets of handrails on the stairs, the lower one for elementary youngsters and the higher one for adults.) Remind me to show you the covered-over gas lights in the auditorium, too.

As I step out of the car, I have to be careful not to step on the dog poop. (See the neighborhood person walking his dog in the yard without a pooper scooper?) Also, watch out for the discarded condoms, broken crack vials, and dirty needles! Just shoo the pigeons away. Neighborhood people throw crackers and bread on the ground here, and the pigeons are so engrossed in their breakfast, they don't move out of the way when they hear people approaching. Rumor has it that the local people resent teachers using their playground and deliberately make this mess. Luckily, it's not winter yet, because starting in December, the yard becomes an ice rink, and one has to hold on to parked cars to safely navigate across it.

Since this yard is not officially a parking lot, no one is responsible for salting or plowing it. For a number of years, staff chipped in and paid for snow removal themselves. It eventually became a nightmare of record keeping and, after a number of secretaries quit the payless and thankless job, plowing was ended and each person now fends for herself or himself. Some faculty members and even some guests, unable to park, have been forced to return home on snow days. I'm carrying a very heavy book bag. English teachers are notorious for carrying home tons and tons of books and papers with them each evening to mark papers and make lesson plans. We are used to carrying most of our belongings with us, even during the school day, because we may use as many as five different classrooms per day (but they are the same five rooms every day). Don't worry about me; I can manage this heavy bag by myself.

Let's head for the elevator on the first floor, even though I am sure that it is out of order. And so it is. (See the "out of order sign" covered with graffiti—probably done by irate students or staff?) Such breakdowns occur very often in this seventy-five-year-old building, and I am used to schlepping up to the third floor to my first classroom of the day. Fortunately, I don't have any physical limitations, but other staff members and students do. Do you? Can you manage?

I know that the broken elevator, once again, will cause severe hardship to everyone with asthma, heart problems, back ailments, broken bones, and other serious ailments. One of our finest chancellors, Dr. Richard Green, the first African American to head New York City public schools, died of a severe asthma attack in May 1988, just fourteen months after taking office.[5] Asthma is a critical health problem, especially here in the Bronx.

It is a common sight at Carter to see asthmatic students gasping for breath as they attempt to walk up five flights of steps in the four minutes between classes. Those who can't make it are destined to sit in the infirmary on the second floor all day or go home early. There is Alicia sitting on the second-floor steps, trying to catch her breath. She always comes early to school in order to give herself extra time to walk up the stairs if the elevator is broken. She is a nursing student, and her classes are on the fifth floor! Stop with me for a minute so I can see if I can help her; she's wheezing badly, and I'll offer to go with her to the nurse (not a licensed nurse—only a nurse's assistant with the responsibility of caring for sixteen hundred to eighteen hundred students, as well as staff). Once there, Alicia will have to decide whether to wait until she feels better or have her parent pick her up, a frequent occurrence.

Working in the infirmary for forty minutes every day (a sixth-period professional assignment?) in addition to teaching five classes of thirty-four students each (that's right—170 students per day), I cover the assistant nurse so that she can leave for lunch for thirty minutes—and I hope that there is no medical emergency on my watch. Almost daily, I have seen the infirmary crowded with students who couldn't walk up the stairs or had tried and given up.

By the way, the Bronx has more asthmatic children than any other borough. "Asthma is the most common chronic disease of childhood, one that strikes the poor disproportionately," says Dr. Elyssa Ely. "Up to one-third of children living in inner-city public housing have allergic asthma."[6] Reports indicate that more trucks, especially diesel trucks, pass through the Bronx than they do in any other borough, causing the worst air quality in the city.

Dr. Daniel Remick, a scientist at the Boston University School of Medicine, adds that "for inner city children, the major cause of asthma is . . . allergies to cockroaches."[7] Cockroaches are a persistent problem in students' homes and schools.

And I haven't yet told you about our coal-heated, mouse-infested building. Wait—I'll get to that later.

Some asthmatic students stay home and call in each day to see if the elevator is working. The constant malfunction of the elevator lasted for only the first seventeen years of my tenure at Carter and finally, in 2002, a new elevator was installed—rumored to cost $1 million! Worse than this outrageous cost was the total loss of elevator service for an entire year. While the old elevator was being replaced, handicapped and asthmatic students were forced to transfer, temporarily, to other high schools. Some called to tell us that the schools they transferred to, ironically, also had frequent elevator breakdowns. There was great excitement and anticipation in 2002 when the new elevator was launched. However, this new elevator also broke down frequently. What can you expect for $1 million?

Back to Alicia. As I help her up from the filthy steps and brush off the dirt on her skirt, I see James approaching. He is an illustrious member (truly) of the custodial staff, and a graduate of Carter. He had wanted to become a New York City policeman, but his mother thought that the job was too dangerous. He is in charge of the distribution of supplies, and with the elevator not working, his arms are weighed down with heavy cartons of books to be delivered to the fifth floor. Of course, James is out of breath with such a heavy load and he decides to take a rest. James had been my student when he was a freshman, and he must have liked my class because for the next three years, he chose to sit in my room every day instead of going to lunch. I do want to point out that since all supplies have to be carried by hand when the elevator is out, you can imagine how delayed supplies are in reaching all the offices and classrooms, but it is not the fault of the supply people.

James offers to escort Alicia to the infirmary; she needs help walking. Finally, I'm on my way to my room on the third floor. As I reach the third floor, I smell paint, and now I can see messy paint cans left out in the hall. I am instantly reminded that this past weekend, New York Cares, a voluntary organization, had come to paint the school. Look at the spilled reddish-purple paint all over the floor and woodwork and classroom doors! There are so many missed areas, and the new coat of paint doesn't begin to cover the dirty gray paint underneath. It will take more than one coat of paint to cover all that grime.

Now, New York Cares is New York City's leading volunteer organization, and it does remarkable work in all the boroughs of New York City. Many corporations and their employees volunteer their time and effort for public service, and one of their annual events, New York Cares Day, has been in existence for seventeen years.

One such day occurred on Saturday, October 8, 2008. According to the New York Cares website, "On that day, more than 8,000 caring New Yorkers . . . took part in New York City's largest day of volunteer service. In just one day they painted hundreds of classrooms and hallways . . . and much more at 119 public schools city wide. Thanks to them more than 88,000 children will find their schools magically transformed into wonderful, vibrant places to learn and grow."[8]

Well, Carter has been transformed all right, but not into a "wonderful, vibrant place"—slovenly and garish would better describe it. When all the walls were dirty and grimy, at least they were uniformly so and there-fore, not obtrusive. Who picked these colors? Teachers certainly weren't consulted. The intentions of New York Cares are definitely honorable, but the results are horrendous, and we will have to live with it. Obvi-ously, an entire high school can't be painted in one day, especially by lawyers, bankers, secretaries, and other amateur painters. The school hadn't been painted in so many years. Why do it all wrong now? Aren't Bronx schoolchildren and faculty worthy of professional painters? Is this how little society values it public schools?

Walking down the hall to my room, I see that New York Cares didn't finish the job. But not to worry—they will be back next year!

I notice that the door to my room has been smeared with paint and my once brass doorknob is now mottled. Before we enter, let me first warn you that, if you are at all squeamish about mice, you should wait outside until I make them scatter; I just stamp my feet on entering my classroom so as to scare (ha) any mice, rats, or roaches that may be await-ing me. The coast looks clear—we can go in now. The first thing I have to do is check the four mouse traps in each corner of my room; sure enough, there is a dead mouse in one of the traps. (What is worse, and I am thankful that I don't have this problem today when I have company along, is finding a squirming, half-dead mouse.) Wait while I call the custodian to come ASAP before my students enter. I hope that this mouse is it for the day, but you never know.

Next, I would like to hang up your coat and mine, but I think you should just carry yours. My old wooden coat closet is falling apart, and peeling flakes of paint always fall on my head, my jacket, and everything else stored inside. I must check the mouse trap set here, too, but it is my lucky day—no mouse. I do keep a sweater here, covered in plastic, because my room, fall and winter, is always cold. This side of the coal-heated building (I'll tell you more about the coal later) is always cold, and the other side of the building is always unbearably hot, obviously an unequal distribution of heat. There are no student lockers in the entire school; they were removed years prior in an attempt to avoid fights at the lockers. Instead there are old wooden, wardrobe closets with sliding doors and low-hanging hooks, another remnant of elementary school days.

No student would ever use these closets; there are no locks, and who knows what lurks inside their doors? Carter pupils wear their coats or carry them around all day. However, when they have classes on the sul-phur-smelling, hot side of the building, they will sweat and otherwise be totally uncomfortable because of the excessive heat and the wearing of their coats. Asking students to remove their coats often becomes confrontational, especially since once removed, students have no place to put them. Teachers, interested in keeping the peace, quickly learn to avoid the issue.

My room is crying out for fresh air; however, if I choose to open the windows, I will confront the seventy-five years of bird droppings mounded on the window sills. I make the decision to open the windows anyway, just an inch, and only for the first-period class. Keeping the windows closed makes the room feel like a tomb. Not that you can look out anyway—the windows have been whitewashed and are permanently opaque. I try not to take in the odor from the bird droppings, but the smell is foul, and eight years after retiring, I can still smell the bird dung. The decision to open the window an inch is a big mistake, and you'll see why later.

I look at my watch; the clocks in my room and in the halls have never worked in all the years that I have been here, and since I teach three classes in a row, it will be almost three hours before I have a bathroom break. So now I will begin my quest in search of a viable ladies' room. Come along with me. The good news is that there is a third-floor women's bathroom and lounge (lounge being a euphemism—no one in her right mind could or would "lounge" in here). I approach with trepidation, and I must warn you, this facility is not a pretty sight.

As I open the door, my eyes search downward immediately, to check for flooding, a common problem. So far, so good. We enter through the small, cramped outer room, where there is a window that is opaque. By the way, there are no screens on any of the windows and pigeons frequently fly in, at their leisure. Over on the left wall is an antiquated, three-cushioned couch with a worn yellow plastic covering. The couch has one leg that bends in. Sitting on it doesn't inspire confidence, and I always avoid it. In the center of this "lounge" is a rectangular wooden desk, with carvings done by hundreds of people over the century. Four matching wood chairs surround the table, and each chair guarantees that you will either get splinters or torn stockings. Sometimes you may even get both. A small bookcase with glass doors and three shelves resides on the back wall. Some "stuff" has been left there forever, and so there is no storage for teachers in this room. That's why teachers carry everything with them as they change rooms throughout the day. The indescribable tile floor is washed occasionally; I personally have seen this done, but nothing can clean seventy-five years of grime and filth, and the worn-out grayish tile always looks unappealing. Some faculty members drink their thermoses of coffee or tea and eat lunch in here, but I am not one of them—my stomach couldn't handle it.

And now comes the really bad part of this bathroom. I am about to enter the small, really tiny, inner room housing two worn-out toilets and a matching sink. First, I must remember to place a chair to hold open the inner door because the lock on this door locks you in but doesn't let you out. Sometimes there is a warning sign posted, but not always. The consequences of being locked in are unimaginable.

Always the optimist, I glance over to the brownish yellow sink to see if this is the day soap is available. No—it is not. Next, I check for the availability of toilet paper. No luck there either. Not to worry—I always carry my own supplies, just in case.

In 1960, when I was a new teacher, I went to one of the first meetings of the newly forming United Federation of Teachers (UFT). The first item on the agenda, set by the older, more experienced teachers, was the continual lack of toilet paper and soap in all bathrooms. Forty-two years later, in 2002, when I went to my last UFT meeting before retiring, guess what was at the top of the agenda? You guessed it—the lack of toilet paper and soap. (Although I have seen tremendous, successful changes accomplished by the union over the years, this problem is one they never solved.)

There is no window, no vent, and no air freshener in this bathroom. The constant foul odor in this diminutive chamber is enough to make one sick. I wish there were a better bathroom to use, but the next closest one is on the second floor, where all the most important administrative offices and the infirmary are located. The staff, all visitors, and all distinguished guests use that abominable bathroom, and to make matters worse, there is usually a long wait.

This second-floor bathroom is the smallest bathroom in the school (no "lounge" here), and it also lacks every conceivable amenity. If possible, it is worse than the one on my floor. One has to use a paper clip to lock the bathroom stall door—if one is lucky enough to remember to carry a paper clip. In order to flush the toilet, one has to use a foot lever, and it takes Herculean strength to accomplish this feat. Of course, there is no window, no vent, and no air freshener in this bathroom either. The only positive thing I can say about this facility is that the women move through it quickly; one does not linger here to freshen up—no chance of that.

And the students' bathrooms are worse! In addition to all the deplorable conditions described above, students have to contend with smoke-filled interiors, bathroom stalls with no doors, fires in wastepaper baskets, and stuffed, overflowing toilets. Many teenagers tell me they avoid the bathrooms and wait until they get home—seven hours later!

Needless to say, these conditions should never have been allowed to exist. This is not a third world country—it is New York City.

I tried my best, as a member of the UFT executive board, along with many others, to get improvements made. We once had an air freshener installed; it was stolen on its first day of use, and none was ever installed again. It may be hard to believe, but there were so many problems and obstacles with which to deal, that after a while we learned to perform triage, to develop a system of priorities designed to save the educational lives of our students. But I wonder to this day how we put up with these dehumanizing conditions. A very dear friend and colleague recently met with some Carter retirees and told them that I was writing a book about our high school. The first thing they said was, "Tell her to write about the bathrooms." And so I have.

I am rushing back to my room because I can see students, although it is still early, waiting at my door. I hope they are not leaning on the wet paint. Lisa wants to open my door, and I hand over the keys, reminding her to make loud noises as she enters the room. Everyone laughs—they all know the tricks. Other students arrive and begin to settle in, most wearing their jackets and placing their book bags on the floor. The first-period bell sounds, signaling the start of classes, and over the loudspeaker comes an announcement to stand and pledge allegiance to the flag. However, there are two obstacles to this simple everyday procedure. In half of all classrooms, the speakers don't work. That half doesn't pledge! While I am lucky to have working speakers, my problem is—we don't have a flag! Sometimes I have a student draw a flag on the chalkboard, but usually there is not enough time. For a while we had flaglike stickers to pledge to, but most of the time we have nothing to look at. I bought a flag once, but it was stolen, and I made no further attempt to correct this situation.

When you practice triage, not having a flag is a minor problem; not having working loudspeakers is a more serious problem. There are times the overhead speakers are used to warn staff about bomb threats or intruders in the school. We used a code: If an intruder were in the building, we would hear, "There is a meeting at Delphi today," and we would lock all our doors and keep away from them. There was a different code for a bomb threat, and when we heard that code, we had to check, surreptitiously, for a bomb in the closets, under the desks, anywhere. As soon as the loudspeaker was turned on, students (who weren't supposed to know what was going on) would yell out, "Is it going to be a bomb or an intruder?" And remember, half of the school never heard any announcement!

It is time to begin my lesson, and just as I start, Jessica screams out, "Mrs. Mayer, I see smoke outside the window!" I know what it is immediately. It is not a fire, I assure everyone—only a coal delivery being made three floors below us. In the late 1990s, more than two hundred schools were still being heated by coal. We have a fireman, a proud Carter High School graduate, class of 1964, who spends his day stoking the coal furnace in the basement of the school. I close the window quickly, but it is too late—many students start coughing and wheezing. I take everyone out into the hall and send those who have asthma and are wheezing and coughing to the infirmary. Although this delivery occurs only a few times a year, combine it with the roaches, the mice, and the overall poor air quality in the school and the Bronx, and you can readily see how terribly the physical environment affects students' education and their lives.

As a member of the school improvement committee, I tried, unsuccessfully for seventeen years, first to get the coal-heated building converted to oil and then, at the very least, to have the coal delivered after school hours. I lost both battles, and so the rooms above the furnace were the recipient of the fumes and smoke that were released on delivery. As the city finances improved, the coal bins were finally removed and an oil heating system was installed, in time for the twenty-first century, but too late for the students of the twentieth century.

Forty minutes after the first bell sounds, another one should ring to signal the end of the first period. But today is a special schedule day, and the bell system has to be operated manually instead of automatically. The person in charge, an administrator, never gets it right, and every special day turns into mass confusion. Honestly, I tried hard, through the school improvement committee, the UFT executive board, and the principal to get someone else to operate the bell by hand, but it was another battle lost. I have been waiting an extra ten minutes already, and while my students are well behaved and are remaining in their seats, out in the halls hundreds of students are crowding together, having left their classes when they saw how late it was. There is a surge of students at my door, and I know that I have to let my students go.

She-who-was-in-charge never learned how to fix the bells and wouldn't allow anyone else to learn how to do it, claiming it was her responsibility. We learned to dread special schedule days, and teachers would contemplate staying home rather than face the utter confusion of the day. She-who-was-in-charge was not a teacher, and that fact proved again that every administrator should teach at least one class a day to be able to relate to what goes on in the classroom. (Today most administrators, superintendents, and mayors in control of schools are business people and have never set foot in a classroom since they were students!)

I hope that my next class, now cut short by twelve minutes, will be uneventful. Here they come, a little wild because of all the confusion in the halls. I commiserate with them, and, finally, my lesson begins. All of a sudden Keisha screams out, "There's a mouse in my book bag!" Her book bag was on the floor, and she had put her hand in it to retrieve her pen and pulled out a mouse instead. The mouse is scampering all over the room, petrified I think, and so are we. I'm not good with mice, I confess, and so I join the girls as they climb on their chairs. The boys just laugh, and I ask Carlos to get the custodian quickly.

I cannot go on with the lesson until Mickey is caught, and so we await our savior. Of course, when he arrives, the mouse is nowhere to be seen. The custodian sets another trap for him, and I try to go on with the lesson, all the while keeping on alert for any signs of the mouse. One of my girls, in her haste to jump on the old wooden chair, scratched herself badly on a large splintered piece and is bleeding profusely all over the dirty, dark brown tile floor. Theresa volunteers to take her to the infirmary, and off they go.

Desks and chairs are so decrepit, accidents occur frequently. Also, for some of the really big and tall students, this old furniture is way too small, and they have to keep their legs stretched out in the aisles. Often, I allow them to just stand in the back or on the side of the room.

Maybe this is the right time for you to see the rest of my classroom. The chalkboard has big holes in it, and I have learned to write around the holes. The windows are the originals; not only do they leak, but they rattle in their warped frames. These old window frames don't hold the windows tightly, and a special needs student, trying to open the window wider, stuck his arm out, and the window fell on him, breaking his arm. You may ask, "Since there are so many problems, what is best in the room?" Easy—*the students!*

After my quieter third-period class, walk with me to the English office to pick up some materials. Only the English chairperson is there; we greet each other, and we are suddenly startled to hear what sounds like a car backfiring. We rush to the window and, since we can't look out (opaque whitewash), we open the window just in time to see men with guns. The noise of the window opening causes the men to look up at us. Quickly we realize how foolish we are to put ourselves in danger, and we hastily close the window and back away. We'll never make that mistake again!

What I have described above is by no means an exaggeration. I wish it were. It is a true, albeit, composite picture of the terrible conditions under which students and faculty worked. Some days were worse than others, but they were all extremely difficult and occurred before, during, and after any learning could take place. Picture all of us under these abysmal conditions and then . . .

PICTURE YOURSELF!

I leave school after 3:00 P.M. and walk to the playground. I can't believe my eyes: The side window of my ten-year-old beige Toyota Camry has been smashed to smithereens!

Looking inside the car, I see that my radio has been cut out and all my wiring has been slashed. A dear friend and colleague approaches and tries to comfort me. She reminds me that at least I still have my car. "Remember," she says, "when anyone who had a red car had it stolen?" How could I forget that? She looks past my car and fixes her gaze on her equally damaged car. Yes, her side window has also been smashed, and her radio is gone too. Instead of crying, we laugh and figure out how to deal with this problem. Our all-too-frequent lament—with outstretched hands—is, "What's the use of complaining?"

As I drive away from Carter High School (I can and do leave the Bronx, but my students can't and don't) with a damaged car, no side window, no radio, small pieces of glass remaining on the seat and floor, the last thing I see are the beautiful yellow and red fall flowers planted voluntarily by Carter students with the help and guidance of an elegant, dedicated, Jamaican English teacher. It is quite a sight to see six-foot-tall football and basketball players planting these colorful flowers inside the wrought iron fence surrounding Carter and beautifying this very ugly, old school building. I chuckle as I drive off and am instantly reminded of Lorraine Hansberry's play *A Raisin in the Sun*. Mama and her family are leaving the squalor of their neighborhood and apartment and at the last moment, Mama goes back to retrieve the small, fragile plant that she has somehow kept alive in the midst of bleak, sun-deprived surroundings.[9] Our students are just like that plant: Nurture them and they too will grow!

In 1999, oil heat replaced coal at Carter H.S.

In 2002, the elevator was replaced.

In 2003–4, the drafty, broken windows were replaced and the encrusted bird droppings removed.

But for a period of twenty-five years, the last quarter of the twentieth century, nothing was done.

It was the worst of times.

II

Defying Expectations

4
Omara—The Orphan

It is easier and quicker to get to know the noisier students than it is to get to know the quieter ones. The student who asks for the bathroom pass and informs you, and the entire class, as to what bodily function must be performed immediately or dire consequences would result, is so different from the shy kid who would rather die than even ask for a bathroom pass! Some students tell you their life stories quickly, and others never say a word. Omara was one who never said a word—until calamity struck!

She was a student who kept to herself, worked diligently, seemed pleased that she was making good progress in reading, and was getting good grades—and never revealed anything personal to me. She was very pretty and wore her dark brown hair pulled back tight. Her facial features were very regular, in perfect alignment, and the severe hairstyle emphasized her natural good looks. She always appeared to be neat and clean, in typical teenage attire, jeans and a shirt—nothing fancy, nothing that stood out. She was absent from school one day, a rare occurrence for her, unlike so many students who are chronically absent and/or cutting classes—and I remember asking her if she had been sick. Instead of just nodding yes or no, she explained to me that she had had nothing clean to wear. She had washed out her clothes, but they hadn't dried in time. I smiled at her sympathetically, but didn't question her any further. Years of experience had taught me never to pry, just listen to whatever they wanted me to know. This was the first time she had revealed anything private-like to me. After this incident, I did notice that she wore and "re-wore" the same two shirts.

On the last day of school before the Christmas vacation, she gave me a small greeting card, signed it "Love, Omara," and kissed me goodbye. I was surprised by her show of affection and thought that maybe she did it in the spirit of the approaching happy holiday season. After all, except for that one talk about her wet clothes, she never really had spoken to me. Now, students kissed me hello and goodbye all the time, but for Omara, this was a first. In retrospect, it was a breakthrough.

I hope by now that I've convinced you that teaching was my calling, but don't get me wrong, I'm no saint. I look forward, desperately, to all the holidays and vacations. Unless you are or have been a teacher, you have no idea how exhilarating and exhausting it is to teach 170 students per day (five classes, thirty-four students in each class). A colleague, a young English teacher from the Philippines, left my school after accepting a position at Great Neck High School, Long Island, where he taught only eighty students per day (four classes, twenty students in each class), and received $10,000 more in salary! Most parents, after spending a day with their two or three teenagers, are worn out—so think of the huge numbers of students city high school teachers meet and deal with each day.

The Christmas break, however, is not a happy one for many students. Their home life often is difficult or even chaotic, and the gifts we shower on our loved ones and the family gatherings we have around the table for holiday fare are not part of their experience. Let's face it; we have commercialized the holidays so much that many people equate gifts with the celebration. And if you don't get gifts, and if your family gathering is tense or nonexistent, you can get very depressed at such times. I worry about many of my students who have told me about their hatred of the holidays. (Omara was not one of them.) All I knew about her was that she had few clothes. She didn't share her holiday plans with me, and I didn't question her.

The first day back after the vacation, kids are very chatty, catching up with their friends and teachers. (What did you get? What did you do?) It is difficult to get classes back on track, but in less than three weeks, the January regents examinations would begin, a week of high-stakes testing.

Omara hardly greeted me, which surprised me because of her affectionate departure eleven days earlier. A *New York Times* picture showed chancellor Joel Klein kissing a young student in a school he was visiting. Letters to the editor appeared the next day, applauding the fact that you could still "kiss" without it being viewed "wrong." Issues of child molestation had led to all sorts of overkill and overboard directives about refraining from kissing and hugging and touching students. I took my chances; after thirty years of students' show of affection, I could not and would not shove them away.

Omara worked diligently, as usual, on that first day back; at the end of the period, she waited for everyone to leave and then spoke to me. I was not prepared for what she had to say, and I still choke up about it as I write about her. Omara asked me if I could recommend a good orphanage for her because her father had been killed in the street, in the Bronx, during Christmas, and she had no one with whom to live. She uttered all this in a matter-of-fact tone—no emotion! I looked at her, and the tears welled up in my eyes. I could not believe what I had just heard. Overwhelmed, I remained silent for a moment—trying to regain my composure, allowing my mind to find the right words. Instinctively, I put my arms around Omara in an attempt to comfort her. She saw my tears and hugged me back and told me not to worry. Imagine—she was comforting me!

I had a free period next, and Omara had lunch. We walked out of the room together, and I managed to say that while I didn't know of an appropriate home for her, I did know of a very caring, nurturing guidance counselor, mother of six, who could help her. Another huge city problem—not enough guidance counselors. They are given hundreds and hundreds of students to guide and often are overwhelmed just by the record keeping for each student. There is precious little time for life's emergencies, and students quickly learn that some counselors offer little or no guidance. They're too busy with paperwork (now computer work).

Although this counselor was not the one Omara was assigned to, I knew that she would drop everything to help a student in trouble. I told Omara that I would accompany her to the guidance office, and she readily agreed to go with me. On the way there, Omara gave me a capsule view, a condensed version of her life, none of which she had ever revealed before. For most of her fourteen years, she had lived with only her father and more recently, lived with him and his girlfriend and her two young children. Her mother had been lost to the street, and she had no contact or relationship with her. During the Christmas break, her father had been shot and killed on the street where she lived. Her father's girlfriend, a woman Omara liked, could not afford to keep her. There were some distant relatives in Brooklyn, but she had tried living there some years earlier and it hadn't worked out. Again, she said the best place for her would be an orphanage. She said it impassively. It was a good thing that we had reached the guidance office; otherwise, students in the halls would have seen me in tears. I just listened to Omara's story but made no comment—what could I say? I barged into the counselor's cubicle (too small to dignify it by labeling it an office), and trying to hold back my tears, I blurted out to her that Omara, a very fine young woman (as opposed to a disruptive student who would have a hard time getting a counselor's sympathetic ear), was having a severe family crisis and was in desperate need of her help. Although Omara was not part of her caseload, she dropped everything, closed the door to her cubicle for privacy, and very calmly promised Omara that whatever the problem, she could help her. (That's why I chose Ms. Donato.)

Omara sat down (I remained standing—no room for two seats), and Omara began to tell her story and ended by asking the counselor to recommend a good orphanage, preferably one in the Bronx, so that she could continue here at Carter High School. Ms. Donato questioned Omara as to her relationship with her father's girlfriend, Jennifer. Omara explained that Jennifer cared for her, but without her father's financial support, she could not afford to keep her. Asked if her first choice would be to stay where she was, Omara almost smiled and said that that solution would be too good to be true. Ms. Donato made some calls—to the Bureau of Child Welfare, the school social worker, and others—and told Omara and me that she would get back to us with information by the end of the day. Did Omara have a place to stay that night? She responded that she could stay a while longer in Jennifer's home.

Omara agreed to meet me at 3 P.M., the end of the school day, and about 2:30 P.M., true to her word, Ms. Donato got in touch with me and said that everything was all arranged. Child Welfare would pay Jennifer to keep Omara with her. Jennifer had been contacted earlier and had agreed to this solution. Omara met me after her last class, and I told her the good news. At first, I think her heart and mind wouldn't accept her good fortune. She had fortified herself to accept the worst outcome, and this happy solution was not what she expected. She smiled, cautiously, and asked for all the details. We then "ran" down to the counselor's cubicle so that she would learn for herself what the arrangements would be. Only after hearing Ms. Donato's words, did she allow herself to flash a big grin and hug us both.

I wish I could tell you that Omara lived happily ever after. (Does anyone?) Not that her life wasn't ever happy, but it was very hard—there was no doubt about that. She continued on at Carter High School through the tenth and eleventh grades, stopping by my room daily for hugs and support, discussing unfolding events in her life and in school. Her living arrangements with Jennifer were good but not perfect. They clashed over what every mother (or stepmother) and teenage girl clash over—boys, boys, boys, studying, clothes, curfew, and so on. In this case, the usual teenage angst was exacerbated, I have no doubt, because of the nonbinding, precarious relationship between Omara and Jennifer. When Omara would tell me that Jennifer was too strict and wouldn't let her out on a school night, for example, I would try to neutralize or counteract the severity of the problem by telling her that if she lived with me, I wouldn't let her out until she was thirty-five and then only on Sunday afternoon for an hour. She would laugh and, putting things in perspective, worked things out with Jennifer to a certain degree.

As her senior year approached, Omara acquired a boyfriend, and, soon after, she became pregnant. Although she liked her boyfriend, she wasn't sure of marriage. She was sure that she wanted to have the baby. Her daughter was born in late winter, a few months before graduation. Up until that point, she had kept up with her classes and schoolwork. My fear was that she would drop out before June. But Omara was made of sterner stuff. Defying the expectations of almost everyone around her, she set herself on her determined path to graduation in June, on time, with her class! She hired a babysitter for her daughter, but she had to take the baby, by bus, to the sitter's home and then take two buses to get back to school in time for her 8 A.M. class. At the end of the school day, she reversed this complicated procedure. Somehow, she worked it out, but it certainly wasn't easy. Several times during the term, the baby had severe asthma attacks and was rushed to the hospital. And then there were the sleepless nights when the baby, like most babies, couldn't tell night from day and chose nighttime to be awake. When Omara did miss classes, upon her return, she asked all her teachers for makeup work. (Some teachers cooperated; others gave her a hard time, as if her life weren't hard enough. Some had strict rules about no makeup work!) Omara herself had asthma, but she forced herself, even when sick, to get on that early morning bus, 6 A.M., carry the baby and all her paraphernalia to the babysitter, take the two buses to school—rain or shine or snow or sleet—sit for all her classes and then go back to pick up her daughter at the end of the day.

Omara went through the most difficult, grueling few months of her life, but she persevered (some days in desperation). Statistically, she should have been a dropout. A lesser person, like me, never would have succeeded. But contrary to expectations, on June 25, Omara graduated on time, with her class! Her father's girlfriend, Jennifer, was there, and holding the baby on his lap was Omara's boyfriend. And I was there too—applauding loudly until my hands couldn't make another clap!

Omara obtained a job in a day-care center, which not only gave her a salary and a career path but also provided her with day care for her daughter. She enrolled in college night classes but eventually dropped out when the relationship ended with the father of her baby. However, she kept on working in day care and occasionally wrote to me and sent pictures. She was a single parent but was coping with whatever the situation required, as it was her nature to do. I hadn't heard from her for a couple of years when a letter arrived accompanied by a picture of her beautiful four-year-old daughter. It was a very cheery letter. She had met a wonderful young man, married him, and was building a good life as a family, in the Bronx. She was back at college, at night, advancing toward certification as an early childhood teacher.

She was happy; she was functioning; and, despite all the obstacles she had to face, despite being a teenage orphan and a teenage single mother, she conquered all the odds against her. And I know that no matter what life throws at her in the future, she'll be able to handle it—because she's a fighter—a winner—and my hero.

(On December 14, 2006, Omara telephoned me. After no communication for several years, she informed me that she was now a proud college graduate and that she owned not only her own day-care center but also her own house—in the Bronx! Didn't I tell you that she was a winner!)

5
Remarkable Ramika

What you noticed first about Ramika was her large, horn-rimmed glasses. You saw the glasses before you saw her sweet, soft-looking face; she had medium brown skin and was of average height and weight. She could have easily melted into a crowd of students, except for those oversized spectacles. They were the kind of frame that, in the movies, an awkward, shy young woman wore until someone (Prince Charming, probably) discovered that, if the glasses were removed, underneath would be found a "smoldering beauty." Was Ramika smoldering? I didn't know.

How can I describe Ramika's life? Not that she confided in me quickly. I would say that it took the first term and well into the second term before she shared some of her troubles with me. She was an average student, which meant at Carter High School and at many city high schools that she passed four or five classes out of six or seven taken each term. It may come as a surprise to you, the reader, to learn that many city teenagers accept the failure of two or three courses per term as the norm. In suburbia, this high failure rate would be a shock as well as a terrible stigma and would warrant a meeting with the student's counselor and parent. In the city, failing a few courses per term is so common that it hardly even raises an eyebrow on anyone's part.

Ramika's passing grades ranged from 65 to 80, and I felt that she tried only half-heartedly to pass her classes; as with so many of our students, there was no great incentive to excel. (Sometimes, no one at home cared about their grades, and so that made it harder for students to care.) Ramika had told me that she had failed social studies because she couldn't understand the teacher or the textbook. I looked over the book and discovered that it was far too advanced for the average student and that it was very out-of-date, typical of many textbooks used in the city schools. However, Ramika felt "lucky" because half of the class had no textbook at all. Outdated books are better than no books, and all academic subject areas suffered from a paucity of books. (Nursing students, preparing for a state exam, would spend hours at our copy machine in the English office—often the only one working in the building—copying pages out of their shared textbooks!)

Ramika had failed Spanish I in her first term but was put ahead into Spanish II for her second term because Spanish I wasn't given in the February term. (By the way, Spanish was the only language offered in a school of nearly two thousand students, half of whom already spoke Spanish.) What were her chances of passing Spanish II when she had failed Spanish I? You can surmise.

Again, this programming problem would never be tolerated in most suburban schools, and yet it occurs over and over again in the city schools. (Suburbia would often run a small class, if it were needed even by only a few students; the city, grossly underfunded, couldn't afford to run small classes.)

I told Ramika that the trick to learning a new language was that she had to go home every night and memorize all the new words and idioms she had learned that day or else she would keep falling behind. She gave me a long, long, serious look and told me, slowly, so that it would register—that it was impossible to study at home because she shared a room and one bed with her three younger sisters. Not only was there no peace or quiet at home, but also there was not a free moment. She did all the cooking and shopping and cleaning because her grandmother was ill and couldn't do it. Over more time, Ramika revealed to me that her maternal grandmother had taken her in, along with her three younger sisters, when her mother "disappeared." I asked what "disappeared" meant, and she explained, reluctantly and painfully, that she hadn't seen or heard from her mother in years. She was a crack addict, and one day she left and never came back. Ramika and her sisters had gone to live with her mother's mother eight years earlier, when she was only eight, and now, at sixteen, she was still living with her. The grandmother couldn't work, was on welfare, and—here's the real shocker, as if things weren't bad enough—they had had no heat or hot water or electricity for the past two winters! The building was in complete disrepair. The people who could move elsewhere did, but Ramika's grandmother, sick and with four youngsters to care for, couldn't afford to move. (New York winters are brutal; in case you're not familiar with our weather, snow, sleet, and freezing temperatures are the norm for December through March and sometimes even into April.)

Ramika did have a social worker, but she had been unable to help. I asked Ramika if I could tell our high school social worker about her plight, and maybe she could contact Ramika's social worker and perhaps, just perhaps, the two of them could make some progress. Ramika was convinced that it was useless to try. So here comes my philosophy: "Ramika," I said, "if you try, the worst scenario would be that nothing happens; but the best case might be that something positive happens and maybe with some luck, you might even get some or all of the services restored." I convinced her to give it a try.

Weeks passed. The winter was almost over, and the family finally got heat, hot water, and electricity. I told her that she had learned a lesson for life: just try. She felt so fortunate. Her family life improved, but only to the extent that when Ramika cooked and cleaned, she now had the bare necessities; however, she still slept in the same bed with her three sisters.

She still had no time or quiet place to study. I was amazed by her conscientiousness and willingness to accept responsibility for herself and her sisters. She knew her priorities, and studying quietly, even in part of a room, was out of the realm of possibilities. (Never mind "a room of her own.") So she did the best she could, and you can better understand why failing two or three classes was not such a tragedy. Her attendance was very good, except when the grandmother's condition worsened or her sisters were sick. She paid close attention in all of her classes because she knew that, once home, she couldn't do anything but be a home-maker. At almost seventeen, she saw a bleak future ahead. She confided in me that she had to keep her younger sisters in school, even if it meant that she had to drop out. Any thought of ever going to college was not only unrealistic, it was totally out of the question.

Ramika had kept her family together since she was a very little girl. That she had successfully assumed all the duties of a mother and father at such a young age was a credit to her tenacity, intelligence, maturity, common sense, inner strength, and diligence. That she made it to her senior year was miraculous. Her ability to defeat the odds and overcome enormous obstacles would work for her in the future—I, a lesser person, just knew! She was already my hero and been so since I first met her.

I spoke to Ramika about going to college, and she called it "an impossible dream." She said that no one in her family had ever gone; no one had even graduated from high school. Not only did she have no money, she had to take care of her younger sisters. I begged her to apply anyway, explaining that maybe there was scholarship money available, for an "outstanding human being." (She laughed.) Maybe her fifteen-year-old sister could help out with the two younger siblings. When Ramika approached her grandmother about college, her grandmother cried and said she would make any sacrifice to send her to college, if there were any way it could be done.

Ramika filled out five different college applications and also applied for any available scholarship funds. Her college essay began, "As a young African American woman brought up on welfare with no mother or father, I would be the first in my family to go to college. If I can attain this goal, then my younger sisters can hope to follow in my footsteps."

Having heat, hot water, and electricity helped keep Ramika's family healthier, and in her senior year, she hardly missed any school days because of family illness and responsibilities. Maybe her grandmother rallied; maybe her sisters helped more. Whatever the reason, Ramika's last year was her best. She managed to make up all her credits and pass all the classes needed to graduate. She was accepted at the State University of New York at New Paltz, a four-year college about an hour's drive from New York City. But there was no scholarship commitment and, without money, there was absolutely no chance of attending that college.

The day of graduation, June 25, was, naturally, the hottest day of the year. We usually held our graduation at the prestigious Bronx High School of Science, which had a much larger auditorium than ours. Although it was larger, it was not prestigious enough to have air conditioning, and previous graduations held there had taught us to wear very lightweight, light-colored clothes, and lots of perfume!

Since no scholarship money had been awarded to her, Ramika planned to look for a job. I was sitting on the stage that day substituting for an administrator who was absent. The sounds from the microphone didn't fully reach the back of the stage where I was sitting, and I couldn't hear everything that was said. Most of the scholarships had been given out previously, on Awards Night in May, so most of the athletes and scholars had received their awards already. But a few are left as surprises for graduation day, and the audience and the recipient learn about it at the same time. A very slim, very short, gray-haired African American lady was called up to the podium. I heard almost everything she said; she had graduated from Carter High School forty-eight years earlier and had majored in nursing. (In those years Carter's nursing program was quite rigorous with a large enrollment, only to deteriorate in later years.) After four years in college and four years working as a nurse, she said that she decided to go to medical school and become a doctor, the first in her family to not only go to college but, of course, the first to become an M.D. This was the third time she had been asked to be a guest speaker at graduation, and this was the third time that she was going to award a full scholarship to a student who showed the greatest promise and was the first one in her family to go to college.

As she spoke, the microphone became more muffled, and I heard her say that she was extremely proud to award this full scholarship to . . . . I couldn't hear the name! The audience went wild clapping and whistling, and I asked the colleague near me who the recipient was. She said she hadn't heard the name either. I was trying to catch the attention of some-one closer to the microphone when suddenly, unexpectedly, I was pulled out of my seat and hugged and squeezed and kissed by Ramika herself. And that's how I learned who won this scholarship. It was a perfect moment in my life and Ramika's, and neither of us would ever forget it.

Did Ramika go to college? Did she finish college? Well, she decided to postpone going for a year so that her sisters would be a year older and better able to take care of themselves. The money was held for her and could be redeemed the following year. That summer she moved out of the Bronx, and I don't know if she ever completed college. But I do know that she was a remarkable young woman and wherever she is, she's doing well—because she's a fighter—a winner—and my hero.

6

Marion—A Rare Gem

It was the first day of classes in September, the second day after Labor Day. The halls were filled with students, armed with new programs, searching out their new rooms and teachers. I noticed a very sweet-looking young girl peeking into my room. She was nervously clutching her program and checking the room number and teacher's name on the door. She entered my room tentatively and was almost pushed aside by more aggressive students in pursuit of the best seats in the room. (For some students, that meant the back of the room, the farthest away from the teacher; for others, a very few, they grabbed the seats closest to the teacher's desk.) Although this class was made up of ninth graders, new to the high school, some entered more self-assured than others. The shy, sweet-looking girl stood out because she had not yet chosen a seat; was she waiting to be told where to sit, or was she waiting to find a seat no one else wanted? I recognized her predicament and waved her to a front row seat near me. She was quietly pretty, with big round dark brown eyes and chocolate brown fluffy hair worn in a soft page-boy style more typical of the 1950s than the 1990s. She was wearing a dark blue flared skirt and a plain white blouse not usual for the first day of high school, where the outfits ranged from tank tops and jeans to jeans and tank tops. She gave me a quick, nervous smile that indicated "thank you" without really moving her lips or uttering a sound.

I told each new class in September that I wanted for them exactly what I had wanted for my own two sons when they were in school. I wanted them to be happy and to learn. I also said that I expected them to show up every day; half of success in life was just showing up, and if they worked hard, I would guarantee their success in English and reading.

Some of my students, Marion being one of them, bought into my philosophy right away. (I could tell by her smile and more relaxed look. Others would need to be convinced—they had the Missouri show-me genes.) Most of my reading students had been labeled failures because of their low junior high school scores; many didn't even have their junior high school diplomas because of their low scores. Many had been left back for two years and still were unable to reach ninth grade reading and math levels (see Chapter 9, "Multiple Intelligences: A Digression"). To me, they weren't failures. How could fourteen-year-old students think of themselves as failures? The city school system had failed them, by not providing the right intervention, but that's another story. What mattered most was the "here and now." They were here, and now I could help them! As she listened to me, Marion looked like she wanted to applaud, but she restrained herself. At the end of that first class, some students lingered to ask me questions, including Marion. In a very low voice, almost a whisper, she asked for directions to the lunchroom, and I sent her along with some other girls who were headed there, too.

Marion came to class every day, usually early. She sat down in front, near me, and began to work on her individualized reading assignments. As the weeks passed, she proved herself to be a rare gem. She was highly motivated and bright and eager to improve. She worked at her own pace, mastering slowly but surely most of the skills she lacked. (This was an individualized reading class, based on each student's clearly diagnosed needs and interests.) Marion never wasted a moment; she worked from bell to bell and would not be distracted by poorly behaved students or false alarms—bells rung either by mistake or by students eager to cause disruptions in the school day. She just continued on. Whatever help I offered, she grabbed. In her introductory writing sample, she revealed that she was an only child, living with her parents and her grandmother. They had come from a Central American republic and spoke little or no English at home. Marion was learning English as a second language, and that helped account for her low reading scores. The harder she worked, the more she learned, and the happier she was. In the beginning, she was too shy to talk to other students and spent most of the term immersed in her books and work, until I made a surprise birthday party for her. It wasn't a big deal, but it was something I learned students really appreciated. Many of them had no celebration at home; certainly, in high school, unlike elementary school where parties were more common, students were unaccustomed to birthday parties. Many stayed home on that day, and to encourage their attendance, I made a fuss over their birthdays.

Marion's was going to be the first party that fall, so she had no reason to expect it. The day of the celebration, she came in quietly, as usual, opened her folder to begin her work, and immediately noticed the card I had left there. As she read it, she flashed me her glorious smile (how I love smiles), and I pulled out, from my closet, birthday balloons and cookies and juice. I told the class to stop working (you can imagine how they hated to do that) while we took time out to celebrate Marion's fourteenth birthday. Everybody sang "Happy Birthday," and two girls volunteered to help distribute the refreshments. Marion's face was flushed from embarrassment and excitement, but she seemed to enjoy the attention. I gave her the leftovers, and she, in turn, gave them to the two volunteers. They thanked her—and kissed her—and it was these two girls who eventually became her best friends throughout her years in high school; they would prove to be very devoted friends through some very tough times ahead.

Marion wasn't only my dream student—she became every teacher's dream student. How could it be otherwise? Her attendance and punctuality were perfect; she paid strict attention in class, took notes on everything, always did her homework, and studied for all her tests. She never misbehaved or acted out or spoke out of turn. An ideal student!

Although she was assigned to my class for only one period a day, she came back on her lunch period to do more class work. She worked as hard in that second period as she did in her first. Others, one-period only students, were amazed!

Over the next few years, Marion, while no longer in my class, visited me daily, showed me her good grades, and would occasionally ask for help or advice. We kissed hello and goodbye, and if by chance we met in the halls, we kissed again, as did lots of students. By the third year, I knew Marion's mother and grandmother well enough to kiss them, too.

My first grandchild arrived at about the same time that Marion became a senior. I was as excited and happy for Marion's new status as she was excited and happy for my new status as a grandmother. I told her that I hoped my granddaughter grew up to be as beautiful a person, inside and out, as she was. Marion and her family bought my new grand-daughter adorable pajamas with matching booties. I tried to accept the gift graciously, but I was uncomfortable receiving it because I knew it wasn't easily affordable for them.

The senior year in high school in New York City is probably the most stressful for even the most confident teenager. In addition to making momentous decisions about their future, they had (and have) the added burden of meeting the new higher standards, passing regents exams, in all major academic areas. (Most New York suburban students pass these exams by their junior years because they have no language barriers and are better prepared, by both the home and school.)

Until the 1990s, a variety of diplomas were offered in New York City. The Regents diploma was given in recognition of the highest achievement, and a general diploma was granted for meeting all requirements for a diploma, but on a more average level. (In the 1930s, my mother graduated with a commercial diploma, which led to a career as a secretary or bookkeeper, as they called accountants in those days.) Both the Regents diploma and the general diploma enabled students to continue their education or enter the job market or the armed services. Marion's graduating class was the first one to need to pass regents exams in order to obtain a diploma. New York City had instituted a "one-size diploma to fit all," and in the history of New York City schools, this high standard was a first. (In reality, one-size diploma doesn't fit all, and my colleagues and I knew that more students would fail to graduate because of this new requirement.)

The New York City Department of Education was the butt of endless jokes and sad tales of bungled bureaucracy at its worst. For years, they couldn't even get an accurate count of the number of city schools under their jurisdiction! In this bureaucratic maze, they imposed these new standards, higher graduation requirements, without first rewriting curriculum and without adequate teacher preparation and training. These new tests were, and are, grossly unfair! Jonathan Kozol, in *The Shame of the Nation*, states that "high stakes testing takes on pathological and punitive dimensions."[1]

What is certain is that for many of the immigrant children who have not lived in our country for long, these new high-stakes tests were stressful beyond belief. Marion was caught in this unbelievable turn of events, her class being the first to require passing the English regents. (Math, science, and history regents would be phased in slowly, in the future.) Passing these new tests in order to graduate scared Marion and many students like her. (The English regents has since expanded from a three-hour test to a six-hour writing test.) Even in New York City's "glorious" past, whenever that was, if ever, there was never a six-hour English writing test.

These new high-stakes tests, for students like Marion especially, presented problems that were nerve-wracking—almost impossible—almost beyond her capabilities. I say almost because Marion had more guts that most linebackers on the football field. She would tackle the problem, no matter what. She would give it her all. Her teachers gave her extra help; she let no opportunity slip by. But the pressure on her was enormous.

She was an only child who was much loved and nurtured and protected. She couldn't bear to disappoint her family by failing this test and not graduating. She was certainly not alone in feeling this intense burden. Our school social worker predicted an increase in suicide attempts by young people placed in this overwhelming predicament. You have to realize that families were planning big graduation parties, relatives were coming from all over, including even from other countries, to celebrate what for many was the chance to attend the first high school graduation in the family. Students' futures were at stake—everything depended on graduation. (By the way, the "one-size" diploma means that even special education students have to earn the same diploma.)

As her senior year progressed, I could see Marion falling apart. She was working so hard, but she was frantic about the possibility of failing and not graduating with her class. She and her friends would walk by my classroom every day on their way to lunch, and I would try to reassure her and all the others that they could and would pass the regents. After all, doesn't hard work and perseverance lead to success? Nobody could be more conscientious than Marion.

When I first read about the new federal act signed into law by President George Bush in 2002, No Child Left Behind, I was astonished that these words belied the fact that more children would now be left behind, not fewer. This new law was poorly thought out and its draconian consequences had never been fully anticipated. Schools all over the country are turning themselves into "testing mills," spending most of their time and money on preparation for mandated tests. Talking about money, NCLB was and is seriously and profoundly underfunded, making the states shoulder the financial burden. NCLB is—without a doubt—the Katrina of education! (See Chapter 14 for more details about NCLB.)

Back to Marion. I was on my way to the English office when I was confronted by a large group of students, Marion's friends. They were crying uncontrollably and couldn't tell me what was wrong. Finally, through the tears, one of them attempted to speak: I could hear Marion's name being repeated over and over, and I knew that something terrible had happened to her. Tears welled up in my eyes, too, and then a young man in the distraught group managed to blurt out that Marion had fallen from the fire escape in her sixth-floor apartment to the concrete pavement below and was rushed to the hospital. They were all on their way there, but stopped to inform me about the accident. When my classes ended, I too rushed over to the hospital and found the lobby overflowing with students. I hadn't realized how many good friends Marion had made during her high school years. Everybody was either sitting and crying or standing and crying. The hospital personnel told us that she was extremely critical, having, among other life-threatening injuries, severe head trauma.

And so the vigil began; more students and more teachers came and went, but her family never left. The prognosis was not good; so much damage had been done to her head. It was almost impossible for her to recover, and if she did recover, how much of her would remain? The days ran into weeks, and the weeks became months. There was still a daily vigil. Her family was always there, but the number of students dwindled, as graduation day came and went. Although Marion was unable to go on with her life, others had to.

What had happened? How did Marion fall from the sixth-floor fire escape ledge? Was she chasing a homework paper that had flown out of her hand, as her family said, or were the pressures of her senior year too much?

Unanswered questions. What I do know is that Marion started making progress, beyond all expectations, defying even doctors' expectations—although not her family's. She began improving after months of operations and convalescence. First an operation on one eye, then the other—then repeated operations on both. She was the miracle girl. She had to learn to walk and talk again, and slowly, very slowly, she got better. She desperately wanted to return to school in September, begin her senior year again, take her regents, and graduate the following June, just a year late. However, she needed further operations in September and home schooling was the only alternative; of course, in typical New York City bureaucratic bungling style, it took months to obtain it.

Marion needed to pass one more test, the Regents Competency Test in history. She had passed the English regents in January and she had to take three more classes in order to complete all her credits. Late fall, she finally returned to high school, extremely frail, accompanied on the bus every day, rain, snow, or sleet, by either her mother or grandmother.

Each day, I would meet these grand ladies in the teachers' cafeteria where they waited patiently for Marion to finish her classes. How heroic they were! That June, Marion's fifth year in high school, she graduated—triumphantly! Her outer appearance had changed drastically: She was thin and her gait was halted; her beautiful eyes didn't focus correctly; more operations were needed, and she had a metal plate in her head. Her body was damaged, but her spirit was undaunted. The real Marion was a fighter with a strong will to succeed; the sweetness and goodness and sensitiveness that had always been there were still there. There would be more operations down the road, but they didn't interfere with her college plans and her goal to become a teacher, just like me, she said.

On the last day of school, in June, I took Marion and her mother and grandmother out to dinner on City Island, a part of the Bronx that looks like a New England fishing village, complete with wooden piers and boats and stores selling bait and related fishing equipment. It was a gorgeous day, in spite of the heavy rain, and was a fitting celebration for such an auspicious occasion; however, it was a bittersweet farewell because we would no longer see each other every day. We promised to keep in touch, but we knew that our time together had ended. It is a teacher's lament—you "grow" them (like the economy), and then you send them out into the world and hope that they are armed sufficiently.

I wish I could end the Marion saga right here. But life isn't that tidy. Marion did, miraculously, attend college in the Bronx and was doing well when suddenly, she had a stroke. Her fragile look was all too real. She was almost completely paralyzed, unable to walk or talk. Once again, she needed to fight back. What is the prognosis? Contrary to expectations? Marion, who has defied all expectations previously, will do so again, I just know it—because she's a fighter—and a winner—and my hero!

7

A Typical American Teenager—
Dominican Republic–Style

The beginning of every term is frenetic, and so it was a few weeks into the term before I realized that not only were two of my students brother and sister, they were also twins. Dora had sparkling eyes, the kind that indicate a healthy glow inside and a spirit not yet killed by either a chaotic home life or a stultifying school system. She was extremely pretty with thick brown hair and a slim figure usually hidden beneath oversized shirts and jeans, a typical teenage outfit. David, her brother, had a twinkle in his eye, not quite a sparkle, because he seemed to hold back a little, whereas Dora bubbled over with enthusiasm.

Dora worked hard without any prodding. Having come from the Dominican Republic a few years earlier, she was eager to learn everything about America and especially everything about a becoming a T.A.T.—"typical American teenager." She had a good sense of humor, was lively, highly motivated, and easy to reach and teach. Her reading needed "polishing," but was below grade level only because of the language barrier; she had grown up speaking Spanish but had a good ear for language. She could hear the subtle differences between her English spoken with a Hispanic accent and English spoken by native speakers. She was determined to sound like and look like a typical American teenager. It became our joke as I tried to convince her that, maybe, becoming a T.A.T. was not necessarily always admirable, but she wouldn't hear of it.

David definitely was the more cautious twin. He did greet me with a smile every day, but he preferred to let his sister do all the talking and ask all the questions. When he did speak, it was obvious that his accent was stronger and his diction weaker than Dora's. I loved both of them; I couldn't help it. They were conscientious, polite, well-mannered, smart, and appreciative. I met their parents, who were very loving and supportive. Dora's mother made beautiful artificial flowers and, on occasion, sent me some. This was a caring family, and one that I wished all my students would be lucky enough to have.

Like other pupils I've mentioned previously, Dora and David often came to my class for extra periods of reading (and peace and quiet, to quote David) instead of going to lunch or study hall. They sometimes popped in at the beginning and end of each day, too.

It was the Friday before the winter recess in February. The last day of classes before any holiday is usually disruptive and difficult. More students than usual cut classes and roam the halls, causing havoc or just adding to the general confusion. The fire gongs go off often and are ignored because of their frequency. In case of a real fire, we would be in trouble. Administrators and teachers and deans, on their unscheduled periods, patrol the halls and chase the delinquent students from floor to floor. Some get caught and are sent to the dean's office.

The bad hall scene gets repeated time after time. A week before a holiday, teachers receive their preholiday memos assigning them to patrols. This is S.O.P.—standard operating procedure—and all attempts to mitigate the chaotic situation never seemed to work. An experienced teacher quickly learns not to teach anything new on the day before a vacation because few students are there to pay attention.

My first-period class had just left and my second-period students were about to enter. David was the first one to enter the room. He grabbed the front seat—he usually sat in the back. I gave him a big smile as I looked around for his sister. She was standing at the door talking to friends. As I looked her way, I saw three or four boys push past her into my room, yelling and screaming at David. These boys were not my students, and the one waving his hand in front of David's face I recognized as a special ed student who was always fighting in the halls. As I approached him, asking him to leave, he swung at David and socked him hard in his face. He kept on hitting David, who was trying to protect himself. Dora ran in and attempted bravely to pull the fighter off her brother while I quickly called for security. They arrived and broke up the fight and took both boys to the dean's office. I was asked to fill out a dean's report and write a description of what I had seen. My report left no doubt that David had not started this fight.

I was sure that my report would exonerate David, but to make sure, I asked other student witnesses to write a statement as to what had transpired. All witnesses were in agreement that David was the victim, not the perpetrator.

Schools were closed during the next week, and I wouldn't see the twins for the next ten days. I thought of calling home to check on David's condition, but decided to wait it out in case he hadn't told his parents.

Dora and David did not attend school on the Monday or Tuesday after the holiday. I checked their names on the absentee sheet and found only Dora's. My eyes caught David's name on the suspension list!

As soon as I was free, I hurried down to the dean's office to find out what had happened. After all, I clearly had written that David had been attacked. The dean was very sympathetic; she knew that this special ed student was a constant problem and was known for always starting fights and getting into trouble. The principal had read the reports but had a uniform policy of suspending both parties in a fight, regardless of blame.

I could understand this policy when it could not be determined who had started the fight, but not in this case. David had never been in a fight before and had no dean's record for any problem. The dean said that "her hands were tied," and she couldn't do anything about it, even though David was also in her class, and was her best student and definitely not a fighter or a troublemaker.

Injustice makes me very angry, and I ran to the principal's office. Fortunately, she was available to see me, and I explained the situation to her. She listened carefully but then explained her policy to me. I told her that, in this case, her decision to suspend David for an entire week was unfair. Although I couldn't get her to change her policy at this point, she did agree to reduce David's suspension to the two days served instead of the entire week, and he could return the very next day, Wednesday. It was the best that I could do, for the moment, but later on I worked to rescind this ridiculous policy. (No need for a justice system—just convict everyone involved.)

Dora and David returned the very next day to school. Dora had been sick and looked pale and weak. David had been terribly shaken by the attack on him. I could see it in his eyes; the twinkle had been replaced by a twitch. His slow walk and bent-over posture were evidence of his pain, both emotionally and physically. His handsome face was black and blue and yellow.

It was months before I saw the twinkle slowly return, and, to tell you the truth, he was never the same. He explained to me that the attacker had knocked into him in the lunchroom and made him drop his tray. David said that he asked the boy to help him pick it up, and the boy cursed him and refused to do so. When David bent down to pick it up—not looking for a fight—the other student kicked it away and threatened him. David decided to leave the lunchroom, but the boy followed him, right up to my room.

That was the story. David thanked me for my help in reducing his suspension, but this entire episode drastically changed him. He was still a charmer, but over the next two years that he remained at Carter High School, he retreated more into himself. Dora would continue to visit me daily, through her junior and senior years. Only occasionally did David seek me out. Once in a while, I caught his eye as we passed each other in the halls, and he would wave to me. His sister would tell me that he was doing okay in all his classes, but not exceptionally so, as she was. She said that he never studied and never did homework but still managed to pass all of his classes. (Many city high school students do not do homework, lacking home pressure and peer pressure.)

Dora was exceptional; she did homework and maintained a high grade point average; in fact, her overall average was high enough to get her into the State University of New York at New Paltz. David hadn't applied to any college; he didn't think he wanted to go and preferred to get a job instead. I tried to get him to apply anyway; he could always defer acceptance for a year. I also knew that once students left the cocoon of high school, navigating the application process later was very difficult, and, without guidance, many would never apply.

Although graduation day is the happiest day of the school year, it makes me cry. You work with students for three or four or five—sometimes six—years, and you know the struggles they endured and the obstacles they overcame, and even though this day is the commencement of their lives, you know it is the end of the relationships you have developed with them. Some come back to visit, once or twice, some will correspond for a few years, but eventually you lose all ties with them. And this is as it should be. They go on with their lives, and as a teacher, you only hope that the school equipped them adequately for their future lives. Did we do right by them? How could we do better?

Dora did return during her freshman year at New Paltz. She was doing well, loved college, loved being away from home, although she did miss her family. She was enthusiastic and happy and proud, and I told her that she was the epitome of a typical American teenager—T.A.T.—her dream fulfilled!

About a year after the twins' high school graduation, David and his father came to see me. David had been working but decided that he wanted to go to college, and he and his father asked for my help in obtaining an application and writing a recommendation. We went to the guidance office, which luckily was open to former students, and began the process of applying to college. He wanted to go to New Paltz, too.

I have not heard from either of the twins since that day. Did they finish college? Are they happy? Are they married—with children of their own? A teacher rarely gets answers to these questions (except in some cases, such as Tamika's, coming up next), but students remain in your heart forever—as fighters—as winners—as my heroes!

8
Tenacious Tamika

I taught in summer school only once, almost thirty years ago. (Once was enough; it was so grueling.) It was there that I met Tamika. It was July 5, the first day of classes, orientation day, and I conducted a tour of the enormous and convoluted five-story building for my group of new students. Some students were noisy, some were quiet, and some were very nervous. These students were all ninth graders, and all of them would be entering Harriman High School in September.

I noticed a very shy teenager, definitely from the "nervous" group. My fear of losing new students in this extremely large building made me act more authoritatively than I ordinarily would. Years later, Tamika, the very shy, nervous teenager, would tell me that she remembered not liking me on that very first day. We laugh about it now, almost thirty years later.

Academic workshops were scheduled for each morning—I taught English and reading—and every afternoon we took trips around the city. We went nearby—to the Bronx Zoo and to the Bronx Botanical Gardens. We ventured out to the other New York City boroughs; we toured Harlem in Manhattan, and we took the ferry to Staten Island. Many of my students had never been out of the Bronx, and they stayed close to me, fearful of getting lost and being left behind. Tamika stuck to me, and so began our relationship that has stuck for all these years.

Although not all the ninth graders in my summer school class were scheduled for my September class, Tamika was. She looked happy to see me on the first day of the new term, and I was glad to see her smiling face as well. (Smiles were always worth points, as I told all my students.)

This Bronx high school was huge. It was built in the early 1970s and could accommodate five thousand pupils. Some would learn to navigate this large system; they could speak up for themselves, even correct mistakes on their programs, a chronic problem; they could arrange for guidance counselor visits and, in general, not get lost in the bureaucracy. However, for a great number of students, coming from small junior high schools, this vast system stymied them.

For example, I once had a freshman who, instead of being scheduled for English 1, was placed in English 8 for seniors. She sat in English 8 for the entire first marking period, and hoped that the teacher would notice the mistake. The teacher did finally notice—after six weeks! By that time, the ninth grader had lost six weeks of instruction in English 1.

The program committee was, as always, inundated, swamped, with hundreds and hundreds of last-minute program changes, and it was common for students to wait many weeks for their correct programs. For the first month of each term, sometimes even the second month, chaos reigned as students sat in the wrong classes and then had to make up the work missed when they finally were placed in the right class.

I informed my students that I had a friend (an aide) in the program office, and I could try to make their program changes move faster through the system. The "non-navigating the system" students, like Tamika, were ecstatic to discover that I could help them and would help them. Tamika's shy demeanor had disappeared as a result of our shared summer school experience, and she had begun to trust me, not only to teach her English and reading but also to help her find her way through the immense city high school maze.

The impersonality and bureaucracy of an enormous high school plays a big part in student discontent and the high dropout rate (realistically, a "push-out" rate). A city high school with five thousand students is way too large, and Mayor Bloomberg has been addressing this problem; however, his replacement of large schools with mini-high schools of one to two hundred students addresses the problem incorrectly and ineffectively. Too small is as bad as too big. But that's another problem (see Chapter 14).

Tamika volunteered to be my monitor, and we did get to know each other very well. I sensed that there were home problems, but, as I told you before, I never pried. Tamika's reading skills improved, and she did move on to higher grade level courses. But she always kept in touch, even during the summer break. Eventually, my helping her with school issues led to her confiding in me about some of her personal problems. She had issues with her stepfather and felt that her mother always sided with him. Her home problems interfered with her schoolwork, and I recognized that she needed professional help. It took time to convince her to seek out a counselor. She finally did, and her mother was called in for discussions and counseling. The problems did not go away, but Tamika managed them better and eagerly awaited leaving home for college in two more years.

I know that Tamika counted on me, as a teacher, sympathetic listener, advisor, and friend, to always be there for her until graduation; however, after spending more than thirteen years at this high school, I decided it was time for a change. I felt bad about leaving my wonderful students and colleagues, but I needed to move on. Students expected me to be there forever, and I knew it was going to be extremely difficult to say goodbye—if not almost impossible.

And then there was Tamika. She was very dependent on me, for academic and emotional support. How was I to tell her about my departure and transfer to another Bronx high school?

I decided to wait until the last week of classes in January, Regents week. Only those students taking a regents exam came to school; my students were coming in for the three-hour English regents (which has now morphed into a six-hour exam—needlessly). Many of my students would check in with me for support and hugs and luck, before the test. I thought that it would be less painful to tell individual students rather than have to face all my classes. Either way, it was so very hard to say goodbye; students cried and I cried.

By the end of that one school day, a petition, addressed to the principal, was circulated and signed by more than nine hundred students, insisting that I remain. So much for telling only a few students.

Tamika was shocked to learn from others that I was leaving. She vowed to leave with me, but I promised her that I would always make myself available to help her. I knew how much she leaned on me, and I hoped that she had grown strong enough to lean on herself now. I gave her my phone number (she already had my address) and told her to call me any time. She took me literally and called—and called—and called—almost daily, including weekends and holidays. I continued to advise her as best I could, and finally, after four years of struggling through high school, Tamika graduated. I attended her graduation, as I had promised, and joined in her joyful celebration.

Tamika was very intelligent, but her home problems had slowed her down and made learning more difficult. She did attend college and found it very hard, especially since she was still living at home. The years passed, Tamika kept calling—and calling. She dropped out of college and then went back. She was determined to be a teacher, like me, she said, and would persevere no matter how long it would take.

It took a long, long time. She continued to call me—and call me—and would visit me at my new school for my birthday and holidays. My new colleagues got to know her very well, and I remember once her car had broken down in front of the school, and faculty members ran out to help her. She was that well known.

Finally, in a desperate attempt to get out of her house, her home problems unresolved and worsening, she moved across the country, enrolled in a community college and got a job in the college bookstore. She called me—and called me—sent cards and always kept in touch. Her life had been hard, filled with ups and downs, but somehow Tamika's tenacity and strong will to succeed always kept her on track. As she kept her bond to me, she kept her promise to herself that someday she would finish college and become that wonderful teacher she was meant to be.

Her story is still not finished. She now has a loving man in her life and is the mother of a beautiful baby girl. In 2008, Tamika moved back to the Bronx with her daughter. Her mother was seriously ill, and she needed to be with her. She did get a job, but frequently has to take off to care for her mother. Her plans include marrying her boyfriend and returning to college to get her teaching degree. I hadn't seen Tamika for ten years, but we met for lunch, with her daughter, at Bloomingdale's in Westchester and quickly renewed our friendship. Her move back to New York City means that I won't have to travel to Tennessee to attend her graduation; she will finish college in New York and I'll be there, just as I was at her high school graduation so many years ago. Tamika is one of a kind—a fighter—a winner—and my hero!

9

Multiple Intelligences: A Digression

I can't wait to tell you about Dolores, Marisa, and Pedro; their stories are coming up next. But in order to write about them, I have to introduce you to (if you don't already have his acquaintance) Dr. Howard Gardner, John H. and Elizabeth A. Hobbs Professor of Cognition and Education at the Harvard Graduate School of Education.

If you have no interest in either fixing or knowing what's wrong with urban and rural education, you can skip the following digression. But I warn you, I may think less of you if you do, because every American, well educated or not, private- or public-schooled or not, has a stake in our society's progress; whether it flourishes is totally dependent on our children, yours and mine and everyone's, native-born or immigrant. We owe it to America's children, all of them, rich or poor, to make our schools the best they can be.

What follows is a very short introduction to the theory of multiple intelligences, with an apology to Professor Gardner for its brevity. If you do choose to read on, you will be on the road to understanding how to make our schools, and thereby all of our students, reach their full potential.

Professor Gardner's theory of multiple intelligences was described in his groundbreaking, provocative, life-affirming, life-altering books: *Frames of Mind*, (1983) and *Multiple Intelligences: The Theory in Practice* (1993). His theory should have sparked a revolution in what we teach our students and how we help them "master the tasks and disciplines needed to thrive in the society."[1] Professor Gardner identified seven intelligences in his 1993 book and added an eighth intelligence in 1995.

1. Linguistic: Sensitivity to the meaning and order of words.
2. Logical-Mathematical: The ability to handle chains of reasoning and to recognize patterns and order.
3. Musical: Sensitivity to pitch, melody, rhythm, and tone.
4. Bodily-Kinesthetic: The ability to use the body skillfully and handle objects adroitly.
5. Spatial: The ability to perceive the world accurately and to re-create or transform aspects of that world.
6. Interpersonal: The ability to understand people and relationships.
7. Intrapersonal: Access to one's emotional life as a means to understand oneself and others.
8. The Naturalist: One who is able to recognize flora and fauna, to make other consequential distinctions in the natural world, and to use this ability productively in hunting, in farming, in biological science.[2]

The profound, notable quotes that follow are taken from Professor Gardner's books, and I use them to illustrate his theory and his beliefs.

"We must recognize and nurture all of the varied human intelligences, and all of the combinations of intelligences. We are all different largely because we all have different combinations of intelligences."[3]

In addition, he stated that "the purpose of school should be to develop intelligences and to help people reach vocational and avocational goals."[4]

And now for the pièce de résistance.

Professor Gardner said, "I am convinced that all seven [now eight] of the intelligences *have equal claim to priority. In our society, we have put linguistic and logical-mathematical intelligences on a pedestal. Much of our testing* [see NCLB] *is based on this high valuation of verbal and mathematical skills . . . but whether you do well once you leave* [school] *is going to depend on the extent to which you possess and use the other intelligences*" (emphasis mine).[5]

Many urban and rural students across the country are either failing the standardized tests or devoting most of their school day and time to passing these tests. In New York City, students are left back by the thousands (against proven studies that show retaining students is not only unproductive, but also psychologically harmful), often two or more times, because they fail to meet the standards. Then they are mandated to spend their summers in non-air-conditioned classrooms, and their regular school day is lengthened so that they can receive tutoring after school to help pass the exams.

When students fail (actually it's the school that fails), the consequences for them are devastating. Their self-esteem is so low, they can barely function either in school or in later life. Schools beat the heart and soul out of so many students, and many never recover; they carry the pain with them for the rest of their lives.

A few years ago, New York City left back over a thousand students—by mistake! This gross error was recognized at the end of October—eight weeks into the term; parents were notified of this mistake and given the option of returning their children to their rightful classes or keeping them back for the year! Can you imagine the trauma for these children? Can you imagine their feelings about school?

Most of the children left back, a few thousand every year, are minority students. NCLB was supposed to narrow the achievement gap in America between black and white, Hispanic and white, and the poor and more affluent (see Chapter 14 for the latest statistics). According to a *New York Times* article, dated November 20, 2006, "President Bush's sweeping education law has resulted in little progress in closing test-score gaps between minority and white students that have persisted since standardized testing began."[6] Not only are we failing to narrow the achievement gap, but in our obsession with these standardized tests, covering only linguistic and logical-mathematical skills, we are grossly overlooking, neglecting, and even abandoning most of the other intelligences. (Many schools have either reduced time spent in gym class and recess or eliminated both entirely.) Why are we committing this crime against our children? It is—once again—"the shame of the nation"!

In 1975, when New York City nearly went bankrupt, most music and art programs were either eliminated or reduced, retaining in high school only required Art 1 and required Music 1 because of severe budget cuts. Thousands of music and art teachers (and foreign language teachers, too) were fired, many with eighteen years of teaching experience, never to be rehired again. In the Bronx high school where I was teaching, built in the early 1970s, before the draconian budget cuts hit all new construction and repair of schools, the fifth floor of my school—the top floor—was built with beautiful skylights in all the art rooms; also, two art rooms with their own kilns were set aside for ceramics and pottery making. Many of the academic teachers, myself included, often "strolled" the fifth floor in order to see the happy, creative faces of our artistic students. It was a breath of fresh air, and enabled us to see many of our struggling academic students—literally and figuratively—in a new light.

In 1975, the skylights were boarded up and the kilns were removed! How sad and depressing it was to walk on the fifth floor and see only leaks coming from the boarded-up skylights.

In the suburbs, not only do the schools offer music and art (and dance and band or orchestra) programs, but also many parents provide enrichment as well. My husband was a high school principal on Long Island (New York), in an upper-middle-class community, where most students not only participated in its outstanding music program, but they also had the best instruments and the best private lessons that the parents' money could buy. I will never forget the sight of the beautiful blond harpist, who brought her own harp to the spring and winter concerts. (It took three nights of concerts each term to accommodate all these privileged students.)

We know that "separate but equal education" never existed. What existed before 1954 and what exists today is separate but grossly unequal schools. In a democracy, schools should be the great equalizer. Instead, they have become the great divider. Is President Bush's No Child Left Behind act, with its total emphasis on academic skills, really the best this country can do for its children, for its future? Schools are blocking the multiple intelligences of urban and rural young people and interfering with their future and their contribution to our society and the world. We are living through a disastrously backward movement in education, and these retrograde steps are occurring all over the country. Once again, it is "the shame of the nation"!

It has been almost twenty years since Howard Gardner's *Multiple Intelligences: The Theory in Practice* was published, and at that time he wrote, presciently, that his concern was with "those who don't shine in the standardized tests, and who, therefore, tend to be written off as not having gifts of any kind."[7]

The talents of many students in America have been written off. If by chance, or miracle, some small number of urban students have their talents developed, it is by their own prodigious efforts, with little or no help from the school or home.

The next three chapters, dealing with Dolores, Marisa, and Pedro, will serve to show you how extremely talented young people almost were written off as not having gifts of any kind. These students were saved, but how many aren't? How many students who might have excelled in other intelligences were never given the opportunity to develop those intelligences? So many students have lost out, and so has society.

It is time to move forward and make our city schools the pride of the nation.

10
Dolores—The Dancer

Unsmiling. Tense. That's how Dolores appeared walking into my classroom for the first time. I said, "A smile is needed to get a seat in my classroom!" It was definitely the wrong thing to say because a large scowl came across her beautiful face. She stopped in her tracks and looked back, wistfully, at the door; it was still open, and she looked like it could be the way out for her.

I saw quickly that I had said the wrong thing, and so I slipped from my opening day trick 1—"Keep the banter light"—into opening day trick 2—"Please sit wherever you are most comfortable." Trick number 2 gets you away from trick number 1—be friendly—when that one doesn't work. (Sometimes my cheerfulness annoyed some students, accustomed as they often were to frowns and scowls.) Dolores hesitated (and I was thinking ahead to trick number 3), when she made a choice of a seat in the back of the room.

She would remain in that back corner seat each day for the rest of the term. Rarely did she ever smile, except for . . . and that's what I want to tell you about.

Dolores was a good student but an unenthusiastic one. She was in my ninth grade reading class and scored just a year or so lower than her grade. Most of my students, but not all, are "unenthusiastic" about reading. All of them had tested below their grade level in reading throughout elementary and junior high school. It is part of our nature to dislike something in which we don't do well. I always told my new students that I was the worst athlete ever, so bad that no one in school ever wanted me on their team, be it volleyball, softball, or even ping-pong. So I do not like, to this day, any sports. But as a teacher, one of my goals was to get students to like reading—for the rest of their lives! Samuel Johnson said, "A book should either entertain or enlighten," and I wanted my students to eventually experience the exhilaration that comes from reading a book they loved and which fulfills either or both of Dr. Johnson's criteria.

Reluctant readers are my specialty. I accept the challenge, and over the years have developed another bag of tricks (academic bait I call it), designed to lure the most unwilling reader. (For many students, "everything is boring" is their typical response to my questions about their reading interests.) So I have devised a simple interest inventory, which I administer on the first or second day of school. In this way, I quickly discover their interests outside of school. (A sample interest inventory is reprinted in Appendix C.)

But Dolores was easy to motivate; she had interests. Or rather she had one overwhelming interest—dance! She loved dancing—she wanted to be a dancer. I didn't have to dig down deep in my bag of tricks for her. She came in each day, pulled out her folder from her class's storage unit, and sat down ready to begin her remedial reading work. No chit-chat, no delaying tactics. In her folder was material that I had placed there related to dance: a magazine article or an entire magazine, biographical sketches of famous dancers, newspaper articles about dancers, obituaries of famous dancers, vocabulary exercises dealing with dance terminology (choreography, dancerly, balletomane, etc.), and movies and TV programs about dance. She couldn't believe that I would cater to her interests. It was really just a small thing. I read newspapers and magazines anyway and found it easy to cut out any articles in which a student might be interested. This simple act went a long way to building up trust and to opening the door to a student's closed mind about reading. I tried to find the exact fit—sports materials were really easy to find, but my lack of knowledge about any sports made me miss the mark on occasion. I once mixed up my student's favorite basketball team with another similar in name and presented the wrong material to him; he read the "wrong" material anyway and was pleased that I had made the attempt to fit the material to his interests. Often, students gave me a second chance to redeem myself and get it right.

Dolores read the articles on dance and seemed to appreciate my efforts, but still she never smiled. Finally, I knew that I had gained her trust when, on a day I had no dance material, she asked me for any reading skills material.

She was caught! She was ready to learn to read better, but she was still not ready to smile—not yet.

During the term, she worked on a research project about famous people, in all walks of life, who had overcome enormous obstacles in order to achieve fame and fortune. She was asked to choose from a list that included dancers such as Isadora Duncan, Twyla Tharp, and Mikhail Baryshnikov and to do research in the school library and the public library. Our library had only four computers at this time, but since many of our students did not have computers at home, the library was the only place that provided access to computers for them.

I introduced Dolores to Mr. Brown, our librarian, and asked him to take excellent care of Dolores because someday she was going to be a great dancer. With that introduction, Dolores, still unsmiling, told Mr. Brown and me that she was going to be in a dance contest the following week and that the winner would get to go to Paris during the summer for an international contest. That sentence was the longest one I had ever heard her speak. I was so excited for her, but she still didn't smile. She continued, saying that she was very nervous, was losing sleep, and couldn't eat. When we left the library, Dolores walked me back to my classroom and informed me that she would not be in school the following Friday because she had to rehearse all day for Saturday's contest. I asked her questions about her dance program and she told me that she had worked out an original routine and, with the help of her dance teacher and a choreographer, had put together a difficult but fantastic, unique performance. She had been working on it for months and had nearly perfected it. I hugged her, for luck, and told her that I would eagerly await the results on Monday. She almost smiled.

Carter High School is a vocational high school, and it specializes in nursing and cosmetology. (However, students must still meet the same academic requirements of a regular, academic high school—in addition to meeting the vocational requirements.) There was no dance program or dance class at Carter High School. How does a student know if she or he has a talent? Certainly not through the curriculum offered in most regular New York City high schools with the obvious exception of elite high schools such as the Fiorello H. La Guardia High School of Music and Art and Performing Arts and the Frank Sinatra School of the Arts. Dance is one of the eight intelligences (bodily-kinesthetic), but it is not recognized by most city schools or the new charter schools or the new mini-high schools.

Why had this talented, highly motivated young woman chosen a vocational school that had no dance program? Was it poor junior high guidance, poor choice on her part, or even poor parenting? (Or was it that Carter High School was the only school that had accepted the student.) In order to be eligible to take the performance test for the few specialized high schools, somebody has to help the student put together a portfolio or a program. That task presents no problem for a middle-class parent, but it can be an insurmountable obstacle in time and money for the poorer parent. As Dr. Gardner says, "No one . . . is likely to develop an intelligence without at least some opportunities for exploration of the materials that elicit a particular intellectual strength."[1] Miraculously almost, Dolores had developed this talent, this intelligence, outside of school, in the Bronx. How many other students, through the years, having no opportunity to develop their talents, have fallen by the wayside?

Monday morning arrived, and since I was teaching three classes in a row, by the time Dolores's class entered, I had already seen sixty to seventy students, and I was not as alert as I had been earlier. It was ten minutes into the period before I spotted Dolores, stooped over, in her corner seat, staring down at her empty desk. I slowly approached the back of the room, stopping to check the work of other students. I tapped Dolores on the shoulder; she looked up, tearfully, but said nothing. It was obvious from her demeanor that the dance recital had not gone well and that she could not talk about it in class. I whispered in her ear that she should wait after class, and I would walk her to her next class. (I did not push her to do her work, and she didn't make any attempt to do it.) I continued making the rounds of all my students, checking their work and stopping to help. Out of the corner of my eye, I checked on Dolores. She was still sitting there—in a semi-catatonic state—and I saw no reason to shake her out of it in front of her classmates. She was wearing her "protective coat," and I wouldn't think of removing it.

She waited for me after class, and I asked her if she wanted to talk. First came her tears and then came the story. I took her into the teachers' "lounge," ostensibly to get tissues, but when I saw that the bathroom was empty, I realized that it would provide the only quiet spot in the whole school.

Dolores was terribly upset, but not because she had lost. The girl who had won, a former friend, had stolen Dolores's dance routine and music.

Somehow she had seen Dolores's performance and copied it with only slight variations. The judges were either unaware of the similarities or chose to ignore them. In either case, Dolores had had no feedback on her performance and only knew that she hadn't won. She spent the weekend crying over the unfairness of it. I asked her how her dance teacher felt about it, and she said that she hadn't discussed it with her; she was embarrassed because of her failure to win.

I told Dolores that she had to do something about this injustice (there went my policy of not interfering). She had to speak up and protest—first to her teacher and then to the judges of the contest. I explained to her that the worst possible outcome would be that they wouldn't change their minds and she would be back where she started, a nonwinner cheated out of her rightful award. But, aha, the best possible scenario would be that she got the judges to change their decision and thereby make her the winner. At the very least, she would know that she had put up a fight; she would get satisfaction out of knowing that she had done her best to correct a wrong. (Alice Walker, in her novel concerning female sexual mutilation, *Possessing the Secret of Joy*, a book I used in my multicultural literature class, reveals that the secret of joy is resisting injustice, fighting back, and not accepting what is wrong.) I told Dolores that although this issue did not involve life or death, it was definitely worth fighting for. Did Dolores hear me? Would she do something about it? I couldn't tell from her misty-eyed sad face.

We didn't get to discuss this situation for the next ten days because the Easter-Passover holiday had intervened. I worried about her over this vacation, as I did for many of my students whose holidays often proved to be disastrous, as I've said. Divided families, hostile families, distant families, no families—all were typical of what many of my students faced during holiday breaks. Not only do many not have a traditional or untraditional Easter dinner with family, many lack heat, hot water, and food, things that the regular school day, five days per week, provides. If you don't work in the city schools, you probably have no idea what life is like for many city youngsters.

Back to Dolores. I had thought about calling her home but wasn't sure if she would consider that an invasion of her privacy or—even worse, if she had done nothing to try to rectify the situation, my calling could just further depress her. I decided to wait it out.

On the morning of the first day back, I had arrived at school an hour early, avoiding rush-hour traffic and allowing myself time to empty my mailbox and get materials ready for what would be the last third of the school year.

More than 75 percent of Carter's students get free breakfast and lunch, indicating that their families or guardians have incomes below the poverty level. According to a *New York Times* article dated September 29, 2009, "The Bronx remained the country's poorest urban county."[2] Often, my students discover that I'm in my classroom early and manage to slip out of the cafeteria and drop in to see me.

Dolores ran into my room, or rather floated in like a ballerina, her face full of smiles-smiles-smiles! I almost didn't recognize her; being happy, smiling, was not something that came easily to her. She had never before come upstairs early to see me. But here she was, and I knew why by her beautiful smile. She and her dance teacher had made an appeal to the judges and produced evidence that proved that the other contestant had stolen her routine. The judges conducted an investigation and declared Dolores the winner! She would go to Paris during the summer for an international dance contest. She was so happy—I was so happy—actually we were both ecstatic. I had to point out to her that she had learned a lesson for life. When a real injustice has been perpetrated, I told her that you can and should try to correct it. There is such glory in fighting back, even if it doesn't always result in victory; however, when it does, the victory is even sweeter, as was her victory!

I would be misleading you if I let you believe that Dolores became a "smiler" after this success. Often she sank back into her depressed, almost catatonic state, wouldn't talk, and barely did her work. She did inform me that she was preparing her dance routine for her summer performance in Paris, and although she was very excited, she was also very tense and nervous and anxious. Did she fear the competition, girls from all over the world, and here she was, from the Bronx? She never discussed these fears, and she never revealed any home problems to me either. From her periods of chronic depression, I had reason to believe that her home life was also a problem. She never mentioned her parents or siblings—ever. I never questioned her about them—I've told you, I try not to pry—until the day I saw what I initially thought were tattoos up her arm, from the wrist to her elbow. Only when she turned her arm over did I notice that what I thought were tattoos were words covering the whole underside of her arm. She had been careful (?) to write only on the underside, not on top of her arm where it would be easily seen. She was explaining something to me and being distracted—without thinking—used her hands for emphasis. When she turned her hands over, the unexposed part of her arm was showing, and I saw the word SUICIDE repeated up the arm—with pictures of a coffin and flowers. I asked her, in as calm a voice as I could manage under the circumstances, "What's that?" She said it was nothing, she was just "fooling around," and she warned me not to report it to any guidance counselor or call home because she would never forgive me.

This was not the first time I was warned by a student not to reveal what could be a suicidal message. I knew that I could lose her trust, but better to risk losing her trust than risk losing her life to suicide. I knew what I had to do; I was horrified, but tried hard to conceal my feelings until the class ended. Dolores left, and I used the newly installed emergency phone in my room to call Dolores's guidance counselor. This new counselor, Lorraine Castro, had been a Carter graduate; for many years she had worked as a paraprofessional at Carter, later becoming a teacher, and just recently, was licensed as a guidance counselor. She knew Carter's students thoroughly, having been one, and what she lacked in pedagogical experience she more than made up for in common sense, intelligence, and compassion. We had been friends for years—my colleagues and I often helped her through some of her courses and exams. As soon as I told her about Dolores, she dropped whatever she was doing and pulled Dolores out of her very next class. She also called Dolores's mom and asked her to get to school ASAP.

Later, Lorraine told me that Dolores was furious at me for reporting "just some silly markings on her arm"—her exact words. She had tried to explain to Ms. Castro that they didn't mean anything. But, after discussions with Dolores's mother and other teachers, it was evident that Dolores was severely depressed. Was this writing on the arm (like writing on the wall) a cry for help? Certainly. Would she have gone through with it? Who knows? What I do know is that it was right for me to report it. I couldn't take a chance.

Lorraine told Dolores that I had done my duty, that it was because I cared so much for her that I had to report the incident. It was determined that Dolores would get psychological counseling outside of school, and inside the school, the guidance department would monitor her behavior daily. A few days later, when Dolores returned to class, she was very cold to me—like ice—and never smiled or looked me in the eye. I never did regain her trust or friendship. Often, she was taken out of my class for guidance sessions, and so I knew that she was getting help.

June arrived, and Dolores stopped coming to school. Was she going to Paris? I didn't know, and I didn't find out until the following October.

It was my last term of teaching. I wouldn't be there in September. (You see why it was so hard to retire—so many needy wonderful students.) My last three years of teaching had been spent commuting from my retirement home in Pennsylvania to the Bronx, a commute of two to three hours each way, depending on traffic and weather conditions. (My family thought that I was crazy and had threatened to institutionalize me if I didn't retire.) I returned to school for a visit in October (so hard to keep away), and as word spread that I was there, students flew out of their classrooms—very embarrassing—and surrounded me in the halls. I had planned to check on Dolores, but she found me. She smiled—she really smiled—and seemed glad to see me. She told me that while she did not win the dance contest in Paris, she had had an unforgettable experience.

Will she be a famous dancer some day? I'm placing my bet on her, and I know wherever she is now, she's dancing. And when she's dancing, she's smiling. After all, she's a fighter—a winner—and my hero.

11
Marisa—with Charisma

Marisa was an extremely talented young teenager with an outgoing personality and uncommon singing ability. She could have been written off as not having gifts of any kind (see Chapter 9, "Multiple Intelligences: A Digression") because of her weakness in math. In high school, math counts exceedingly high; in life . . . ?

Marisa was, maybe, four feet ten inches tall; she weighed, maybe, ninety pounds. But, no maybe about it, with her long black wavy hair and huge dark eyes, she was very beautiful. You had to notice her immediately because she sort of danced happily into the classroom each day. She made friends easily and talked to everyone whether she knew them or not. She had a good sense of humor and was full of life. I liked her right away. You couldn't help but like her; her smile was contagious, and everyone felt better in her presence. Talk about charm. She had been in my room only for a couple of minutes when she volunteered to help give out supplies. If students were talking, she asked them, politely but firmly, to quiet down and pay attention. Amazingly, other students, every one of them bigger than she, followed her instructions. She was a force to be reckoned with, as they say.

As I got to know her and was better able to assess her skills, I realized that, although she would score high on the interpersonal and musical intelligence scale (see Chapter 9), she was in trouble on the logical-mathematical scale. She told me that she had always struggled with math and was terrified of the New York math regents competency test (RCT) that had just been put in place as a graduation requirement. Before 1994, no competency tests were required to graduate with a local diploma.

In order to graduate, she had to pass this test, the first of what would come to be called "high-stakes tests." She really wanted to sing and entertain people, but she didn't want to get out into the real world without her high school diploma. Her essays in my English class were filled with her fears about not graduating, not only disappointing herself, but also her mother, grandparents, and boyfriend, who expected so much of her.

What could I do to help her? Mostly, I listened to her laments and tried to build her confidence as well as her skills. She worked like a demon in my class and all others. She stayed late for tutoring; other teachers freely helped her, too. She was such a special young lady, so polite, so full of life, so highly motivated—and so willing to try her best to graduate. With great determination and perseverance, she was able, eventually, to pass the social studies and science RCTs, albeit with the lowest possible passing score of 55. However, she still needed to pass the English and math RCTs.

The dropout rate in New York City and in cities across the nation is very high. Even before so-called higher standards (see Chapter 14 for discussion of higher standards) the cities had failed to graduate about 50 percent of their students. Statistics vary, but not by much, and the highest dropout rate is among minorities. Many, many students stay for a fifth year, and sometimes even a sixth year, to try to obtain a diploma. What follows may seem like a lengthy digression, but I feel it is important for you, the reader, to understand the hypocrisy behind the so-called—here I go again—higher standards.

We, the teachers, knew that the dropout rate would only increase with these "higher standards" and the mandate that there would be only one diploma offered—a Regents diploma. This mandate was to be phased in during the late 1990s, but as of 2010, it is still not completely phased in. We were not alone in predicting a declining graduation rate; the New York City Department of Education must have come to the same conclusion, and soon after the adoption of "one" type of diploma for everyone, they decided that we could maintain the "appearance" of high standards by providing something called "component re-testing" (CRT) for those students who failed the Regents more than twice and had obtained a score between 48 and 54. For these students, the below "55-ers," this special test was administered in May over five days. It was a watered-down version of the Regents and was therefore almost impossible to fail. Giving it in May guaranteed a higher graduation rate in June. Teachers received training for CRT, on how to get the slower students to pass this ridiculously easy test. Initially, CRT was given only to those who failed the English Regents, but results were so good, there was a big rush to get CRT in math and social studies too. So much for so-called higher standards!

Marisa passed, of course, the CRT exam in English and received credit for the English Regents. In her senior year, she needed only to pass the math RCT; however, CRT in math was not available yet. She decided to take the last two required math courses during the summer before her senior year and thereby fulfill the six math credits required for graduation.

Here comes a big glitch. Marisa became pregnant in her junior year. She had been with her boyfriend since ninth grade, and she planned to marry him and graduate on time, despite the anticipated arrival of her baby in September of her senior year. Between her mother's help and a babysitter, she would manage to finish school. Going to summer school and making up six math credits would make her senior year that much easier.

Pregnancy agreed with Marisa, and she seemed happy. She consulted with her counselor, who made sure that Marisa was armed with the correct summer school course cards. Guidance counselors are swamped with hundreds and hundreds of last-minute summer school requests in late June because so many students fail so many courses and exams. (The suburban high schools have more guidance counselors and much lower case loads than the city high schools, and they also don't have the high failure rate to deal with, so they have smoother sailing both in June and September.) In September, New York City guidance counselors are once again swamped with program changes as a result of summer school grades. Many students don't get their corrected programs until October—sometimes not even until November!

Our high school did not offer summer school, and Marisa had to attend another Bronx high school. When summer school began in July, in a non-air-conditioned building, of course, Marisa was nearing the end of her seventh month. She was such a plucky young lady; undaunted by her pregnancy or extreme heat, she attended summer school religiously. She wrote to me during that summer, told me how she had never missed a day, and had passed her first math test with a 65. She never complained about the heat or pregnancy. Some of my colleagues were teaching in that summer school, and they complained bitterly about the sweltering, unbearable humidity and high temperatures. It was one of the hottest summers ever. One of my friends knew Marisa and was amazed that she survived this ordeal.

Well, she not only survived, she conquered. She danced into my room on the first day of school in September and waved her successful summer school report card right at me. We hugged and kissed, and I congratulated her on the successful completion of all math requirements. She had gained thirty pounds, and at four feet ten inches, she looked like an adorable roly-poly teddy bear. She was a week away from her due date; she planned to take two days off and come right back to school. I was amazed at her tenacity, but I also knew that her senior year would be extremely difficult. If she knew the problems ahead, she never let on. Marisa stopped in to see me each day of that first week back except for Friday, the last day. I missed her visit and was worried all weekend. Had she given birth? Was she okay?

On Monday morning, early, before 8 A.M. classes, Marisa came into my empty room, slowly, very slowly, definitely not dancing. There was deep pain on her face and she was no longer roly-poly. She blew a kiss to me and sat down, very carefully, and told me what had happened.

Friday morning, she awoke early with a terrible backache. She was determined to go to school, got dressed and was about to leave home when her water broke. Her mother rushed her to the hospital, and her little Angel was born Friday night by Caesarean section (at the last moment, the baby breeched). The hospital discharged her on Sunday and—lo and behold—here she was in school on Monday! I told her that I was going to call a taxi and send her home. (It was already ninety degrees and climbing higher.) She refused my offer and my help. She said she had to be in school; she couldn't miss a day because she would fall behind, and she had to graduate in June. She just had to!

That morning her mother had tried to keep her home; her boyfriend tried also, to no avail. She went to all her classes that day and the next and the next. All her teachers were amazed. (By the way, Angel's pictures showed him to be as beautiful as his mother.)

Well, I would like to tell you that there was smooth sailing ahead for Marisa, who so deserved it. But sailing was not to be smooth. Rough waters intervened.

Although Marisa had taken and passed her last two math classes in summer school, she was programmed, incorrectly, to take them again. Summer school grades come in late and, as I told you, programs aren't corrected sometimes until October or November. Marisa wasn't overly concerned because these two courses just had to be dropped; it wasn't like she was missing classes that she needed, or so we thought. When she finally met with her counselor, in October, her counselor discovered that the math courses she had taken in summer school were the wrong ones. It wasn't her counselor's fault. The mistake was made by the summer school counselor. It seemed that when Marisa arrived at summer school, the math classes she needed to take were filled up, and the counselor, with no access to Marisa's Carter High School records, no computers then, just reprogrammed her for other math classes. Marisa had taken the wrong classes and would need to take the right classes, now, in October, five weeks after regular classes had begun. Marisa's guidance counselor was shocked. I was shocked, and so was Marisa. We took the case to the principal. You guessed it—she was also shocked, but said that there was nothing that could be done to rectify the mistake. Marisa had gone to summer school, seven months pregnant, passed the wrong courses and would now have to fit in two more classes in her already crowded senior program.

The tears welled up in my eyes for the unfairness and injustice done to this amazingly resilient young woman. Marisa, seeing my tears (by now you've grown accustomed to my tears?), comforted me, thanked each of us for our concern, and proceeded to go ahead and enroll in the correct math classes.

As I predicted, it was a very difficult senior year. Marisa tried to do everything; she came to school every day; she ran home at 3 o'clock to care for her baby and very often, she stayed up all night with her colicky baby. But, still, she forged ahead.

Now comes some good news. In June, Marisa passed all her classes, including those two math classes. But, here comes the bad news: she did fail the math RCT. Since this Regents was given on the last testing day (math being quicker to mark than English or social studies), students find out if they failed it only the day before graduation. It is a heartbreaking day since no one can attend graduation without fulfilling all require-ments. (One year, there were riots outside of the building where gradua-tion was held, perpetrated by irate families whose sons or daughters couldn't attend graduation and were notified only the day before.)

Marisa's family was devastated, but she herself took it stoically. She would come back again in September. She didn't want to go to summer school again, not because of her bad experience—she was over that, though I wasn't—but because she wanted to be home with her baby.

Now, at the beginning of this chapter, I told you that Marisa was a gifted singer. Although musical intelligence had not been nurtured in school, Marisa had sung in a church choir and over the years had performed at nursing homes and churches and hospitals. She helped organize a chorus at Carter, with the help of the one music teacher we had (for almost two thousand students). Sometime before Christmas, she planned a winter concert for the school, and she was to be the guest soloist. She did all the work for this special event, even making sure that all my classes were invited. (Not all classes get to see a performance because our auditorium was too small. Remember, Carter High School had been built as an elementary school seventy-five years earlier.) I was thrilled to be invited because I had never heard her sing and I knew how much singing (one of the eight intelligences) meant to her. As she introduced her solo, she made me stand up (I didn't want to do it) and told the audience that her song was dedicated to me. "My cup runneth over," as they say. Once again, the tears welled up in my eyes and Marisa saw them and told me not to cry, that I deserved this honor—further embarrassment!

Did she solve all of her problems? No. Did she fight as hard as she could to obtain her diploma? Yes. Did she succeed? Well, I wasn't going to be there the following September as I finally, very reluctantly, retired, but I told Marisa that component retesting in math—the easier version of the math Regents—was to be offered that fall term. I knew that Marisa would be there to take it, and I was certain that she would pass it. I wouldn't worry about her, because, you can see for yourself, she was not a quitter; she was a fighter—a winner—and my hero.

12

Pedro—The Piano Player

Some of the most profound conversations that I ever had with my closest colleagues occurred in our non-air-conditioned, decrepit basement lunchroom. (I tore my hosiery every day on the broken wooden chairs that served as lunchroom "furniture.") Although these devoted teachers taught English, as I did, we often lamented the lack of music instruction, not only in our school, but in so many city high schools. The assistant principal in charge of English, another of my heroes, put in endless hours, days, and weeks trying her best to bring music into our school—and it wasn't even her "job." Since 1975, when the city was near bankruptcy, music, art, and foreign languages— considered "frills"—were cut from the curriculum, and, as I told you before, most music, art, and foreign-language teachers were fired. For the last thirty years, the only mandated music course was a one-term-one-credit music appreciation class. One of our two music teachers had "recycled" himself and had become a librarian (and he had a PhD in music), and the other one, an older gentleman, remained to teach the required music class to fifty students per class, five classes per day—a total of 250 students seen daily. Academic classes were "capped" at thirty-four students, but music, a nonacademic frill, overflowed with fifty students, and half or more were often special education students. (In special education classes no more than fifteen were allowed.) Any music teacher, even Leonard Bernstein, would have been overwhelmed. Our poor, worn-out instructor, Mr. Blume, was forced to take off three days each term, when report card grades were due, just so that he could get all his marks entered on marking sheets. Can you imagine teaching 250 teenagers per day?

Of course, we had no band and no instrument instruction. Many students came to Carter High School unaware of this situation and were greatly disappointed. However, there had been a brief time, in the late 1980s through the early 1990s, when live theatrical performances and music and dance permeated the lives and souls of Carter High School students. These were the "Camelot" years!

The principal had asked me to head a committee that would be entrusted to spend $300,000 over a period of three years for anything outside the regular curriculum, targeted essentially for "frills." This "Rewarding Success" grant had been given to our school for reasons that were never made clear to us, but nevertheless we heartily welcomed it.

The committee's choices were easy; we just filled in what we saw as gaps in our students' education. For these three years we brought life to Carter High School. We hired professional musicians to introduce the entire student body to all the instruments in the orchestra, and also to expose them to all forms of music. In addition, for the first time, students could receive instruction, after school, on instruments of their own choice. (Within a very short time, these students formed a band and put on performances in our auditorium for everyone to enjoy.) The Alvin Ailey Dance Troupe was hired and performed live on our own stage—after we paid to repair the stage floor. We took hundreds of students to Broadway theaters, sat in the best orchestra seats, and saw such shows as *Phantom of the Opera, Les Miserables, Fiddler on the Roof, Cats, Miss Saigon,* and *The Nutcracker* at Lincoln Center. I will always remember that one of the theaters, newly refurbished, had soft, velvet-like seats, and students admired their luxuriousness. I told these excited teenagers that the seats should be plush; after all, they cost sixty dollars. One fine young lady turned to me and asked, "And how much did the ticket cost?" Often, after the performances, theatergoers approached me and complimented my students on their exceptionally good behavior. Maybe they had worried when they saw sixty minority high school teenagers enter the theater?

On graduating, these students who participated in the Rewarding Success Program all said that they would remember these performances for the rest of their lives. By the time Pedro entered Carter High School, not only had the Camelot years ended, but there were no students left who even remembered those grand old days.

Carter High School was one of the oldest city high schools, and hidden in some old closets were damaged school clocks, old desks with inkwells, and even, believe it or not, spinning wheels. Lo and behold, in a closet housing worn and torn discarded social studies textbooks that had been thrown all over the filthy floors, was a broken-down spinet piano—untuned, of course, limping on a broken leg, and abandoned many years earlier.

One of my homeroom students, Pedro, was asked to help carry books to this closet, and he told me about the musty, antiquated piano. His passion was music, he said, and he always wanted to play the piano. His family couldn't afford to give him lessons, and he had hoped he could learn to play in high school. He was shocked when he discovered there was no elective music program at Carter, and this school was the only one that had accepted him! He asked me if it were possible for him to play that broken-down piano for the ten-minute homeroom period when only attendance was taken. He said that he would check his attendance with me every day and then go play. He had thought up the whole plan and was so excited, although I knew giving him a key to the closet with almost fifty years of dust and dirt and leaving him there alone would not get approval easily. But you should have seen his face when I said that I would try.

There was another homeroom in that classroom where the piano had been stored; coincidentally, this room was the old music room where, before 1975, students did receive music instruction. I asked this homeroom teacher if he would mind if Pedro went into the closet, by himself, every day to play the piano for the ten-minute period. I would vouch for his good behavior and trustworthiness.

Now, some teachers feared doing something out of the ordinary or feared repercussions from the administration. But Pedro and I were in luck because this fine social studies teacher agreed to the arrangement. To this day, I am grateful to him for his understanding and flexibility and the chance he gave Pedro.

So began Pedro's ten minutes of piano playing every day. Before piano playing, Pedro's attendance was sporadic, but with the advent of his music practice each day, he kept up perfect attendance. (We know that offering art and music in the schools might be just the panacea for improving attendance for many students.) I asked the overworked and overwhelmed old-time music teacher to determine if Pedro really had talent. Mr. Blume went into the closet and was astonished after hearing Pedro play. He could not believe that Pedro had never played before and recognized that this young man had enormous talent. Knowing that this high school would never meet the needs of Pedro, Mr. Blume promised to make inquiries about getting him transferred in June to a Manhattan high school of music.

Mr. Blume went with me to the principal and asked if it were possible, using private donations, to get that broken down piano fixed and sent to Pedro's home. She was very sympathetic to our cause, and she too promised to make inquiries. In the meantime, Pedro zoomed into my homeroom every day—flashed me his gorgeous grin—and zoomed out for his ten minutes of joyful practice. I will never forget that smiling face (you know how I like smiling faces), and I regret never having heard him play.

But—there is always a but. Things went smoothly until the end of the term in January. Beginning in February, there would be a new homeroom person, and I only hoped that he or she would be as understanding as this last one was. He wasn't! He said that he couldn't take a chance doing something so off-beat. I tried to convince him that Pedro was decidedly on beat, but I couldn't get him to agree. I guess I asked him more than a few times because, eventually, he reported me to the assistant principal in charge of the closet (i.e., the social studies assistant principal), and he, in turn, reported me to the principal for "harassment."

She called me down to her office; I had never obtained her permission to allow Pedro to play in the closet, fearing a negative response. But, once again, this principal was very understanding and even felt bad about the situation. Although she did not chastise me for allowing Pedro to play, she did say she could not allow it to continue. However, all wasn't lost. She had made some progress in throwing out the piano. I had to tell Pedro the good news and the bad news. The good news was that if his church would request the piano, it could be sent there; Pedro could practice there and, later on, the church might be able to donate the piano to a "needy parishioner." The bad news—he couldn't practice in school anymore. He was heartbroken about the bad news, but was buoyed up by the thought of getting a chance to play at his church and maybe, eventually, his home.

I was thrilled to see Pedro zoom into my room the very next day and greet me with that same great grin. He informed me, proudly, that he and his mother had spent the day before moving their living room furniture around, keeping a wall empty for the eventual arrival of his piano. I explained to him, with a heavy heart, that making room for the piano was very premature. He refused to listen to me, convinced that he would obtain the piano, especially since I had never failed him before.

It was a piano nobody wanted—and nobody used. It was almost totally dilapidated. Some notes didn't play: the sounding board may have been cracked. Only to Pedro was this piano as good as a Steinway baby grand!

I wish that I could tell you that the piano, at the very least, went to Pedro's church and that he was able to practice there; however, I regret to inform you, the bureaucracy won. As far as I know, in 2010, that broken-down piano is still there in room 324's dirty book closet—unless it has reached the garbage by now. Pedro's living room wall remained bare for the rest of the term. In June, Mr. Blume was able to get Pedro transferred to the Manhattan School of Music where his talent was recognized and nurtured. The following year, Pedro called me and Mr. Blume and invited us to his first solo recital. Mr. Blume was able to attend; I couldn't, but Mr. Blume reported back to me that Pedro had made great progress and performed brilliantly. His new piano teacher praised Pedro's talent, perseverance, and self-discipline. I did send a congratulatory note to Pedro.

It hurts me to think of that bare wall in Pedro's apartment and to realize how close he came to missing out on the most important life-affirming part of his education. It hurts me even more to think of the thousands and thousands of students—not only in New York City, but in all the cities across this nation—who are being cheated out of being all they can be. NCLB addresses only two of the eight intelligences; millions are spent on remediation of academic failures, but little or nothing is spent on the development of the whole child, on his or her unique talent or gift. "Human fulfillment" does seem to come from the process of discovering, developing, and contributing our unique potential to society.[1]

We have cheated—and are continuing to cheat—so many young people out of developing all they can be. It is "the shame of the nation"!

For Pedro, I know that wherever he is, he is making music—because he is a fighter—a winner—and my hero.

13
Bridging the Gap

There are so many other Bronx students that I could tell you about. Would you believe that a young man, our valedictorian some years ago, admitted to a few of his teachers, near graduation day, that he had been homeless for the last year of high school and had been living on the New York City subway, keeping warm and sleeping on the train?

Then there was a female student of mine who showed great talent as a basketball player. Title IX in 1972 had made more funds and opportunities available for girls and women in sports, and Keisha benefited from this more equitable law. She became eligible for a college basketball scholarship; however, the night before the tryout for the award, she and her family were evicted from their apartment. Keisha spent a cold, damp night, sitting on her couch in the middle of a Bronx street! But—not to worry. She did get herself to the basketball competition and she was awarded a full college scholarship.

I have to tell you about Alicia, too. When she was a ninth grader, she told me that her dream was to be an astronaut. That was all I needed to know. I think the poet Langston Hughes was talking to me when he asked readers to bring him all their dreams.

While Alicia was in my ninth-grade class, I tried hard to find reading materials dealing with the space program for her. For the next three years, when she wasn't in my class any longer, she would stop in to see me, and I would pull open my desk drawer and hand her all the articles, magazines, and tapes that I had saved for her, relating to her astronaut

dreams. Her smile alone was worth my effort. Sometime before her graduation, she gave me a plaque that I have kept on my desk at home all
these years that reads "Teachers Make Dreams Happen." Did she
become an astronaut? I don't know, but I'll put my money on her.

You should also know about Donald, a more recent student of mine.
He was a very large fellow, six feet two inches tall and over 250 pounds,
and his reputation for being verbally and physically threatening preceded
his arrival in my class. He was absent for the first three days of the new
term and came late to class on the fourth day. I greeted him with a smile,
naturally, and made no mention of his absence or lateness. Later on in
the term, when we got to know each other better, and he was working
well, he asked me why I hadn't either yelled at him or *sent him packing*
on the very first day that he had come to class. I told him that he probably
would have cursed me out and left—never to return again. (He agreed
that that is what he would have done and said that most teachers would
have been glad to see him go.) I said to him, "I believe that no student,
no matter how disruptive or poorly behaved, ever came to school to
fail." He looked at me curiously, thought for a moment, and said, "Did
you learn that in college?"

No, my dear Donald, wherever you are now, I didn't learn that in
college; I learned it, over the years, from my students and I used it to tap
into their better selves. Most of the time, it worked!

And then there was Robert. He was a brilliant young African American male who loved learning, took the most difficult classes, was an
outstanding student in my multicultural literature class, accepted every
challenge and won a full scholarship to Bowdoin College in Maine. In
his junior year in college, he transferred to Amherst College in Massa-
chusetts; there he majored in political science and hopes one day to
"bridge the gap" between blacks and whites. After graduating from
Amherst, he won a scholarship to Oxford, England, and the last time I
heard from him, he was pursuing a doctorate. We're going to hear from
him—he's a younger Barack Obama—but even if we don't, you now
have met some of my ordinary but spectacular students who, in their
own way, have made the world a better place—and will continue to
do so.

Are Bronx students really "as bad as they say"?

III

Losing Our Way

14

Deception, Dismantling, and Demise of Public Education

O h, what a tangled web we weave, when first we practice to deceive." When Walter Scott penned these famous words, could he ever have known that over two hundred years later, he would be describing the destructive forces in education today? In all good conscience, I cannot conclude my book without commenting on and detailing what I believe are ill-conceived, deceptive, fraudulent practices in education today that, although ostensibly attempting to solve educational problems, are, in actuality, impeding, hindering, distorting and even thwarting the very goals we seek to accomplish, namely, a sound education for every student. In 2002, No Child Left Behind became the most dramatic expansion of the federal government's role in public education since the passage of President Johnson's Elementary and Secondary Act of 1965, part of Johnson's war on poverty, another war not won! This spuriously written, defective dictum was inflicted on America by former U.S. education secretary Roderick R. Paige and former President George W. Bush in January 2002. It is essential for you, the reader, to know the history behind this law that is dismantling and demolishing and demoralizing our public education system today. Please read on.

When George W. Bush was governor of Texas, from 1995 to 2000, Roderick Paige was the superintendent of Houston, Texas, schools. In 1995, at the end of the first year of Mr. Paige's tenure as superintendent, 74 percent of tenth-grade students at Houston's Austin High School failed the Texas math test; however, by 2000–2001, six years later, the year Paige retired, only 1 percent of tenth graders failed—an impressive statistic, right? It was called a miracle and was attributed to Mr. Paige's policy of using sound business policies and holding principals responsible for results. Furthermore, in 2002, Texas bestowed exemplary status on this very same Austin High School. But here it comes—according to the *Washington Post*, November 8, 2003, in a report by Michael Dobbs, one year after receiving this exemplary award, Austin High School was downgraded to low-performing—the lowest possible rating.[1]

So what happened?

According to Robert Kimball, the former Houston assistant principal who helped expose the "Texas miracle fraud," the secret of doing well on tenth-grade tests is not to let the problem kids get to the tenth grade. (Don't be shocked.) In 2001, Austin High School had 1,160 students in ninth grade, but had only 281 tenth-grade students a year later. Students were held back—almost 900 of them—for failing one course, and some were forced to repeat the courses they already had passed.[2] (Easy to get 99 percent passing rate this outrageously deceptive way.) And what lesson did this fraud teach to the almost 900 left-back ninth graders? "Oh what a tangled web. . . ."

In addition to this testing fraud, more than a dozen Houston high schools were caught up in a scandal about the reliability of their dropout rates. Sharpstown High School, in Houston, officially reported a 0 percent dropout rate, and Houston received, in 2003, the first $1 million Broad Foundation prize (Broad Foundation is a private philanthropic organization) for being the best urban school district in the United States.[3] It was the local television station, KHOU, who uncovered the dropout reporting scandal at Sharpstown High School. Sharpstown administrators had changed the withdrawal codes for at least thirty students to make it appear that no one had dropped out in the 2001–2 year. In reality, 27 percent of Sharpstown students left without graduating. A state audit revealed that most students who left school should have been coded as dropouts, and state officials concede that Sharpstown High School numbers were "purposefully" falsified.[4] Katie Haycock, director of the Washington-based Education Trust, a nonprofit group that supports strict accountability standards, said that "dropout rates are notoriously unreliable in Houston and across America."[5] (And yet, extremely high stakes are riding on these dropout rates.)

It was Mr. Roderick Paige, the superintendent of Houston schools, who had initiated this accountability policy based on what he had learned at the Houston-based American Productivity and Quality Center, which provided training courses for executives of Fortune 500 companies. This accountability policy, widely practiced in business, rewarded principals with either bonuses or demotions based on student performance as measured by dropout rates and test scores. When this high-stakes policy was implemented, to no one's surprise, dropout rates declined enormously and test scores skyrocketed. Principals received bonuses of $10,000 and earned top accountability ratings.[6] (New York City gives principals $25,000–$50,000—allowing for inflation and the higher standard of living in New York, I guess.) Shamefully, fraudulently, Houston became the political springboard for the ascendancy of Roderick Paige to the position of U.S. Secretary of Education, and his creation of No Child Left Behind has been the official education act across America since 2002. Much of Mr. Paige's most cherished accomplishments, including the narrowing of the achievement gap between white and minority students, rests on Houston's manipulated data. "It's all phony, it's just like Enron," said Linda McNeil, a professor of education at Houston's Rice University.[7]

The policies that didn't work in Texas, and that haven't worked in the rest of the United States either, became the basis for the policies instituted in NCLB. The rewards for success and penalties for failure were built into this act: Business policies were turned into school policies—a fatal flaw! According to NCLB, three years from now, in 2014, 100 percent of all students will have to be proficient—that is average—in math and reading. Even without the law's surefire temptations to manipulate scores for financial gain (why should educators be less susceptible to temptation than our bankers and Wall Street executives?), a layperson, a noneducator, could readily see that the basic goals of NCLB were not only unrealistic but totally undoable—no chance! Achieving 100 percent literacy will never be doable as long as America remains a nation of immigrants, has a huge poverty gap, and strives to educate everyone. By the way, the official description of NCLB is "an act to close the achievement gap," and since there is a strong correlation between high academic achievement and high income, states must help high poverty schools meet the same academic standards as non–high poverty schools.[8] This "bridging the achievement gap" is a political hot potato that will always resist implementation. Former New York governor George Pataki, during his three terms of office, from 1995 to 2006, consistently and repeatedly vetoed extra funding for New York City's high-poverty schools, as do governors across the country who don't dare risk "offending" their constituents in non–high poverty school districts. (It would constitute

political suicide to take from the rich to give to the poor, and few politicians would tackle this problem.) To understand the enormity of "bridging the achievement gap," see Table 1, "Some Harlem-Scarsdale Gaps"
(page 133).[9]

And here comes the coup de grace, the knockout blow that leads to
all the deceptive practices that are employed in the name of NCLB.
States must set their own standards in reading, math, history, and science
for all students in each grade level and create tests that are aligned with
these standards. Schools must also make adequate yearly progress, or
AYP, as it is called, like machines making more goods each year—
attainable in factories with products, not in schools with kids. In addition,
schools will be graded by results of standardized tests as well as by AYP,
and will receive their very own report cards.[10] (Report cards will be
discussed later in this chapter.) That's all that counts in this law—only
that which can be measured by results of standardized tests and AYP.
What happened to everything else in the curriculum? What happened to
art and music and science and social studies and foreign languages and
physical education and economics and computer technology? Are these
subjects no longer important?

So here's the problem: Since each state creates its own standardized
tests (fifty states = fifty different tests), and since there are such high
stakes involved (loss of funding, schools closed down, principals fired,
teachers and students displaced, etc.), there have been no problems in
making each state's test easier, every year.[11] Principals and other administrators and teachers get their bonuses, and the school gets its federal funding. And the parents and students and community are hoodwinked into
thinking progress is being made.

By using New York City as my model, I can show you, in reality,
nothing virtual about it, what NCLB has actually accomplished or, for
want of a better word, disaccomplished (my coinage), as it descends its
slippery slope of deceit and destruction. New York City, just like Houston, has swindled the public—parents, teachers, students, citizens, and
noncitizens alike—about the true results of NCLB and New York's
dumbed-down standardized tests.

First, a little background information. In 2002, the New York state
legislature gave the new New York City mayor, Michael Bloomberg,
control over the entire New York City school system through 2009. The
billionaire mayor has an MBA from Harvard Business School and is the
founder and owner of Bloomberg L.P., a financial software services company. (Notice the lack of any educational expertise.) Mr. Bloomberg

quickly appointed Joel Klein, graduate of Harvard Law School, antitrust lawyer and former chairman and chief executive of Bertelsmann, Inc., one of the world's largest media companies, as New York City's Schools chancellor. (Notice, again, the lack of any educational expertise.) Together, these two men, noneducators, set out to reform the city schools as quickly as possible. Mayoral control was set to expire in 2009, and was supposed to be reevaluated at that time; however, with no evaluation, it was recently renewed through 2015, at Mayor Bloomberg's forceful urging, despite devastating New York City results on the federal standardized tests, the National Assessment of Educational Progress, NAEP, which is considered the gold standard of all standardized tests. Although NCLB allows each state to devise its own tests, this federally administered test gives the same test to everyone and is therefore the most reliable and valid and accurate of all standardized tests. (NAEP began service in 1969; it is a congressionally authorized project of the National Center for Educational Statistics and is part of the U.S. Department of Education's "Nation's Report Card.")[12] On this gold standard test, New York City has shown almost no improvement between 2003, when the mayor's reforms were first introduced, and 2007. In fact, the new math scores, as published in the *New York Times* on October 15, 2009, show that not only are math scores falling short of goals set by the city, but that students made more rapid gains on math test scores in the seven years from 1996 to 2003 than in the six years from 2003 to 2009, after NCLB was put into effect.[13] The federal test, NAEP, also shows that no progress was made in closing the achievement gap between whites and blacks and Hispanics,[14] a key feature of NCLB and Mayor Bloomberg's reforms (see Figure 1, " 'No Child' Law Is Not Closing Racial Gap") (pages 136–37). What is even worse, even more egregious and heartbreaking than the abysmal scores and statistics, is the fact, yes fact, that states, especially New York, have actually lowered the difficulty of their tests to avoid loss of funding, loss of bonuses, and other penalties mandated by NCLB (see Figure 2 from Sam Dillon, "Federal Researchers Find Lower Standards in Schools," *New York Times*, Friday, October 30, 2009) (page 138).[15]

And here is news that is even more devastating: Although black and Hispanic elementary, middle, and high school students all scored much higher on the federal test than they did thirty years ago, most of these gains were not made in recent years but during the desegregation efforts of the 1970s and 1980s. That was well before the 2002 enactment into law of NCLB, the official description of which is (I'll remind you again), "an act to close the achievement gap." According to the NAEP test, as reported in 2009, 50 percent of white fourth graders were proficient in math compared with 25 percent of Hispanics and 19 percent of blacks, contradicting results from the New York state tests, which show a much smaller gap.[16]

Javier Hernandez, a journalist for the *New York Times*, reported on September 14, 2009, "that if you botched most answers on the New York State math test, you still passed. Seventh graders who correctly answered just 44 percent of questions were rewarded with a passing grade. Just three years ago, the passing grade was 60 percent. In math this year, 86 percent of students passed the test (with 44 percent or higher), but the lowered passing scores have provided fodder for skeptics or anyone paying attention"—please oh please pay attention—"who believe that the state has made it easier for struggling students to pass."[17]

In New York City, which supposedly has shown some of the largest gains, Mayor Bloomberg has used these (deceptive and therefore meaningless) scores as evidence of his successful leadership of the schools and rewarded 97 percent—unbelievable—of all city schools with As and Bs on the Department of Education's report cards last year, 2009.[18] Only 79 percent received As or Bs in 2008. (Remember, schools have to make their AYP or lose funding; so in 2010, I guess 100 percent of all schools will get As and Bs.) However, at more than 50 percent of the schools that received an A on their report card this year, more than half of the fourth graders were below New York State standards in reading, tests which are still so much easier than the federal test.[19] Mayor Bloomberg, on the campaign trail trying to capitalize on raised scores, sent out thousands of e-mails celebrating the higher fourth-grade math scores but never mentioned the low scores on the eighth-grade math tests and the low grades on the fourth- and eighth-grade reading tests. If you don't pay attention, and so many people don't, you may accept his devious devices as signs of success. Mr. Bloomberg's giving of As and Bs to 97 percent of all schools, over 1,500 schools, is a hoax, a fraud being perpetrated on all New Yorkers as well as other people who should be paying attention and should know better, including President Barack Obama and Secretary of Education Arne Duncan. To see how big the hoax really is, see disastrous test results for July 29, 2010, in Figure 3 (page 139). "For the 2009–10 academic year, only 25 percent of city elementary and middle schools received A's, down from 84 percent the previous year, when many more students excelled under easier standards."[20]

The huge gulf between the phony, dumbed-down state tests and the valid federal exams put former chancellor Joel Klein in a peculiar (I call it fraudulent) position because he had staked everything on the state exams, tying them to consequences such as teacher and principal bonuses and the city's A through F grading system for schools. By the way, New York City distributed nearly $30 million in bonuses because test scores supposedly improved significantly in 2009, even though they actually didn't.[21] I almost forgot to tell you that the Broad Foundation, established by entrepreneur and philanthropist Eli Broad, another business leader, gave the city $1 million for being the best urban school district in the country in 2007—just like he did in Houston in 2003. Mr. Broad says that his mission is to transform K–12 urban education through better governance and management.[22] I'm amazed that such rich business people toss around so much money without checking the accuracy and evidence and honesty of standardized test results. They don't pay attention; why don't they pay attention? It's mind-boggling.

Mayor Bloomberg, in his huge $102 million campaign bid for a third term as mayor (even though he had previously pushed through the law for two-term limits and then overturned it), ran a deceptive, shameful, disgraceful campaign based on what he said were improved test scores and higher graduation rates. Diane Ravitch, the eminent education historian and research professor of education at New York University, wrote, "The city says the rate climbed to 62 percent from 53 percent between 2003 and 2007; the state's Department of Education, which uses a different formula, says the city's rose to 52 percent, from 44 percent. Either way, the city's graduation rate is no better than that of Mississippi, which spends about a third of what New York City spends per pupil."[23] Meredith Kolodner, a *Daily News* staff writer, stated on September 23, 2009, that Mayor Bloomberg does not have his facts straight and, according to a study done at Columbia University's Teachers' College, "Mayor Bloomberg's boast on the graduation rate is misleading."[24] (I'll remind you that K. Hancock, director of the Washington Education Trust, said that "drop-out rates are notoriously unreliable in Houston and across America," which obviously includes New York City.)

In October 2009, the *New York Times* reported that Diane Ravitch, originally a strong supporter of mayoral control, but not any longer, believes that the NAEP results for New York, the gold standard test, "is a documentation of persistent dumbing down by the state education department and lying to the public."[25] She also says, "What [the New York State test results] amount to is a fraud."[26] Now, this article appeared in the *New York Times* on October 14, 2009, and on November 3, 2009, three weeks later, Mayor Bloomberg won another term. People are not paying attention!

Are you getting tired of reading about all these appalling, dishonest test scores? I'll switch over to telling you about mayoral control of schools, although by now you should be reaching your own conclusions or, at the very least, you should be rethinking some of your hard-held beliefs. Eleven big city school districts took part in the federal NAEP test, and guess which were two of the lowest performing cities? Well, one was Cleveland, Ohio, which coincidentally (?) had mayoral control, and the second lowest was Chicago, Illinois, which also had mayoral control. It shouldn't surprise you to learn that the two highest performing cities, Austin, Texas, and Charlotte, North Carolina, do not have mayoral control.[27] In 2009, Arne Duncan was appointed secretary of education by President Obama and left his position of superintendent of Chicago schools, a position he had held for eight years. Did Mr. Duncan know that under mayoral control, during his tenure, Chicago schools were one of the lowest performing schools on the NAEP test? If he did, I don't understand how he could have gone to New York City to urge the New York legislature to renew the law that grants control of New York City public schools to Mayor Bloomberg. (And so they did.) Mr. Duncan said and I quote, "I'm looking at the data here. . . . Graduation rates are up—test scores are up—by every measure that's real progress."[28] Unreal, isn't it?

A few months later, in October 2009, talking as they say, out of both sides of his mouth, in response to learning that states have been redefining proficiency down, Mr. Duncan replied, "At a time when we should be raising standards . . . more states are lowering the bar. We are lying to our children."[29] Well, if Mr. Duncan can say that, he has to recognize that NCLB encourages lying to our children (and to all Americans), and he should be doing everything in his power to stop the lying and cheating. Just look at what happened in February 2010 in Georgia. State officials announced that "191 schools—10 percent of Georgia's public and elementary and middle schools—will be investigated for possible cheating on state tests. It was the second time in as many years that the state's testing program had come under fire."[30] Mr. Duncan should stop the presses, so to speak, stop spending billions of taxpayers' dollars on NCLB as well as another $4.3 billion venture called Race to the Top, that only will perpetuate more fraudulent practices. (More about this "Race to the Top" later.)

When Margaret Spellings of Texas became U.S. secretary of education, following Roderick Paige, she continued to push for NCLB along with its system of penalties and rewards. Didn't she ever stop to look at the unworkable, scandalous system of rewards and penalties that has resulted in the dumbing down of states' tests in order to reap the rewards and avoid the penalties? Didn't she have a staff that might have noticed the reports of widespread cheating? At least Mr. Duncan, the successor to Mrs. Spellings, is one step ahead of her. He has seen the reports of the lowering of the difficulty of the states' tests every year, but, still, does not do anything about it. Where is the strong, moral leadership that is so clearly needed? There is no doubt that the business model, with its high-stakes system of penalties and rewards, has failed in education. And if you look at the economy, it has failed in business too. The irony is that those who believe in numbers and measurement of everything have ignored the findings of well-established research and statistics in order to further their own interests. In Mr. Bloomberg's case, he staked his reputation on improving the city schools, and he will do it by hook or by crook.

As I am completing this final chapter, Mayor Bloomberg has just announced that Joel Klein has resigned as chancellor of New York City schools, after eight years on the job. Along with this surprise resignation, Mr. Bloomberg simultaneously announced his appointment of Cathleen P. Black, the chairwoman, formerly president, of Hearst Magazines, as Mr. Klein's successor. Ms. Black, like Mr. Klein, has no educational background and will need a waiver of requirements from the state education department.[31] Here was an opportunity to select a professional educator, or at the very least, someone who had a background in public education, someone who wasn't an elitist. Mr. Bloomberg, obviously, has paid no attention to the low standardized test scores of this past summer, June 2010. Nor has he paid attention to the widening achievement gap between blacks and whites. He still doesn't recognize that after nine years of two businessmen running the schools, maybe he should have hired a professional educator this time.

Who helped Mr. Bloomberg select Ms. Black? Not United Federation of Teachers officials, not Council of School Administrators officials, not parent association representatives, not state education department officials, and not even Mr. Klein. In fact, Mr. Klein "did not know who his successor would be until Monday, the day before the announcement."[32]

Merryl Tisch, the chancellor of the State Board of Regents, has this to say: "I didn't know Joel was leaving, and was surprised when Mr.

Bloomberg broke the news to me around the time of the 3:15 P.M. news conference unveiling Ms. Black as the new chancellor.''[33]

So with whom did Mayor Bloomberg consult?

State law requires that all school chiefs have at least a master's degree and a professional certificate in education, as well as three years' experience in schools. Because Ms. Black has no such certification, she needs a waiver from the state education department, same as Mr. Klein received.[34]

Is Ms. Black really the best choice to run New York City schools? Petitions with thousands of names were sent to the state education department to try to prevent the department from granting a waiver to Ms. Black. As this book goes to print, a compromise has been reached and a second-in-command, an educator, has been appointed. Immediately upon accepting this concession, Mr. Bloomberg announced that there would be only one boss! To whom was he referring?

Another one of Mayor Bloomberg's and Chancellor Klein's signature initiatives is small-school reforms, another failed enterprise, although you wouldn't know it from the accolades this initiative receives from these men. According to Diane Ravitch, "Within the space of a few years, Chancellor Klein had closed two dozen of the city's large high schools and opened nearly 200 smaller secondary schools,"[35] an unbelievably large number. New York has a decade-long history of opening small schools, but the pace skyrocketed in the past seven years under Bloomberg and Klein. "The New Century Initiative" was designed to provide the city's students with small, effective high schools that would help them meet high standards of academic and personal success. The New York City Department of Education and three private foundations—the Bill and Melinda Gates Foundation, the Carnegie Corporation of New York, and the Open Society Institute—together invested $30 million, initially, to transform large comprehensive high schools into multiple small schools. The Gates Foundation increased its donation to $100 million over the last few years. New Visions for Public Schools manages this initiative in collaboration with New York City schools. In 2002, thirteen small schools were opened in the Bronx alone[36]—a staggering number, first of all, because there was no scientific evidence that smaller schools could do a better job; second, there was no successful model to copy; and third, rushing into opening thirteen new schools in the Bronx, without careful planning and reorganization, was doomed to failure.

In 2003, newly retired, I was rehired to work part-time as a mentor in ten of these new, small schools. It was my job to work with totally inexperienced, new Bronx high school teachers of English who were teaching fellows and participants in Teach for America. They had been recruited from all over the country. For most of these participants, teaching was a second career choice, and they were promised either a free or subsidized master's degree if they would work in the most difficult schools in the poorest areas of the city for a period of two to three years. Common sense would tell you that placing inexperienced people in the most difficult schools, when experienced teachers and administrators couldn't handle the job, was never going to work. These new teachers, with no preparation except for a chaotic summer program, began teaching full-time, learning on the job and, in addition, taking two or three courses per term for their master's degrees. New York City and other big cities, such as Los Angeles, hired these totally new and unprepared people. Many of them left after one or two years, or sooner if they couldn't survive. Some took their two years' training to the suburbs, where only experienced teachers would be hired and which offered much better pay and much better conditions. Many left teaching permanently. One recent study, cited by Dr. J. V. Heilig of the University of Texas and Dr. Su Jin Jez of California State University, indicates that by the fourth year, 85 percent of Teach for America teachers left New York City.[37] I saw firsthand what rushing to open so many small schools, without experienced principals or teachers, really accomplished or "disaccomplished." Let me tell you about my experiences mentoring in these small schools.

Although the small schools opened in September, ready or not (not), the mentoring program did not begin until November, another wrong move and one guaranteed to produce new teachers, who, after three months on their own, were exhausted, stressed out, and unproductive, mainly because they didn't know what to teach or how to teach or even how to deal with teenagers. I do want you to know that the young interns I worked with were very fine people, hard-working and intelligent, who sincerely wanted to be good teachers. My first assignment, three months into the term, was to one of the oldest high schools in the Bronx that had been divided up into five mini schools, one on each of the five floors. (Coincidentally, it was the school I referred to in an earlier chapter where I had "kidnapped" a child who had been sitting outside.) Each of the five schools had a special theme—in name only, because no teacher or administrator had any expertise in these theme areas. For example, in the High School for Interior Design and Technology, there were no new or old teachers who had any experience in these areas. It was a bogus theme, designed to influence parents and students to apply and was a hoax perpetrated throughout the school system.

What I found were five nonfunctioning small high schools, where everyone was working hard, but the level of teaching and student learning outcomes were abysmally low. Everyone seemed to be drowning in bureaucratic "daymares"—nightmares that occur during the day. I was assigned to five new English teachers who literally and figuratively grabbed me and held on tight for the entire school year. (See letters of appreciation from my interns on pages 140–41.) There were very few experienced teachers, since most had left when the school was closed. The mostly new administrators were not master teachers themselves, so they were of little help in training new teachers who had no student teaching experience, no adolescent psychology courses, no method courses—none of the basics. The administrators had been quickly plucked from their old schools and were overwhelmed designing and implementing a comprehensive but small high school. There were no special education teachers but there were special ed students, and my interns were teaching them as best they could, without any guidance, and with little success. Of course, it was illegal to teach full classes of special ed students without a special education license, but there were so many flagrant violations, this was just another one that was overlooked.

In spite of a large number of security guards, who were totally unsupervised, students roamed the halls and stairways and when confronted by a principal, ran down to the next floor, another small school, where the next principal there chased them also; the principals spent a great deal of their time just trying, unsuccessfully, to get students into classes. By eleven o'clock, after attendance was taken, many students left the building and hung around outside. When I asked security guards why they didn't keep students in the building, they replied that it wasn't their job to restrain students. The five mini schools were really nonfunctioning; often my interns had only a handful of students in class, and not the same handful from the day before.

Most important, everyone in the building was working under dangerous conditions. This old high school had a loudspeaker system that originally sounded throughout the school, reaching all five floors at once; however, since there were now five different schools, with different themes, one loudspeaker did not fit all the special needs. So, instead of installing a sound system for each floor, the loudspeakers were turned off totally, never to work the entire year that I was there. Therefore, there were no fire drill announcements or any warnings of danger, such as bomb threats or intruders in the school. There was no way to alert, warn, or evacuate the entire school building in case of an emergency. When I questioned security officers about this potentially deadly situation, they assured me that, if needed, they would run through the halls and knock on doors! I spoke to the new principals, and they told me they would look into it. The school was a calamity waiting to happen. Everybody was in danger. I seemed to be the only person who was outraged. Fires broke out in the student cafeteria on the fifth floor a few times, and the cafeteria staff ran to put them out—but what if? Why didn't the fire department ever check this Bronx building?

My five interns survived the first year, somehow, but other mentors' interns didn't; not even the lure of a free master's could keep many of them here. That was a big high school turned into five smaller ones, and I'm describing problems that were only the tip of the iceberg. Probing deeper would take another book. (You should have seen, or maybe you shouldn't have seen, expensive new math books torn up and thrown all over the floor by students in classes with new teachers who were unable to control their students and who were receiving no help from administrators.) It wasn't the new teachers' fault.

My second year as a mentor brought me to another part of the Bronx, to a brand-new two-story high school with only two new small schools. This building was sparkling and beautiful with skylights on the top floor spreading sunshine throughout; however, it too was staffed by new teachers and new administrators. Although the halls were quiet and students were in classes, the quality of teaching and learning was very poor. Once again, I was grabbed not only by my interns, but by almost all of the new staff, eager for advice and help. I met a wonderful young physical education teacher who had been recruited from outside the United States. (The city sent out scouts to go around the world to bring teachers back to New York City—at what cost?) However, on her appointment to this new school, she was astonished to discover that there was no gym. She had to improvise by using the halls or whatever else was available. A young male math teacher, also recruited from another country, was struggling to teach physics to ninth-grade special ed students. The new principal, with no science background, had written a new science curriculum and decided that physics should be taught in ninth grade, instead of twelfth, to special ed students. The math teacher was not even licensed in special ed, never mind physics—another flagrant violation. Unbelievable, right?

One more tale of woe: This school had a beautiful new library, and it was well equipped with tons of new books sitting in unopened cartons. These cartons would remain unopened for the entire year that I was there because . . . there was no librarian! (At the old building where I worked the previous year, four of the five mini schools were denied access to the main library—five principals having turf battles constantly. A principal should be the central person in charge of the school building and having five principals or even two leads to confusion and chaos as well as unbelievable expense.) What I saw here were distraught teachers, administrators, parents, and students. Everyone in these small schools was ill equipped to open and work in a new school without the careful preparation, planning, and professional expertise that were obviously needed. One of my wonderful, extremely hard-working interns was told, on the very first day of the new term in September (I was appointed in November, once again, as were all the mentors), to order $50,000 worth of new English textbooks. She had no English chairperson or any other experienced English teacher to ask for advice. Everyone was inexperienced, and so she did the best she could; however, when the $50,000 worth of books arrived, she realized they were too difficult and not appropriate for her students. Not only was all that money wasted, but the students had no books. It was not her fault!. And Chancellor Klein had the audacity to say, speaking at the National Press Club in Washington in 2009, that, "the root cause of test score disparities was not poverty or family circumstances but subpar teachers and principals."[38] He and the mayor rushed to set up these schools with no chance for success and then blamed the staff! By the way, Mr. Klein always blames the teachers—publicly. Everything is their fault; he accepts no blame!

One of these two new schools was closed at the end of its first year, for academic failure. But they did have fire drills. And more than one hundred furious ninth graders and their furious parents and overwhelmed new teachers, in the midst of a master's program, had to search all over again for a new high school. Worst of all, these ninth graders didn't receive their ninth-grade education. How were they to manage in tenth grade? (Why the other new school wasn't closed is a mystery because they didn't accomplish anything either; however, not to worry, the following September, the closed school was replaced by a new one, with a new bogus theme and a new staff, totally inexperienced.)

Multiply what I saw here (my weekly committee meetings with other Bronx high school mentors corroborated what I experienced) and you will have an idea of the Bloomberg-Klein small-school initiatives. Even the Bill and Melinda Gates Foundation, after donating more than $1 billion to create and support small academies over the last five years, has grown "impatient at the uneven results of breaking big schools into small ones and have withdrawn ALL their funds."[39] The Gates Foundation is now concentrating on teaching: Maybe it should have done that first and not wasted $1 billion. (Maybe billionaires shouldn't be involved in making educational policies? What are their credentials for doing so?) However, Bloomberg and Klein are still opening new small schools despite evidence that they are not working. Unfortunately, they see what they want to see and won't stop to evaluate or check for results or obtain any feedback.

What follows are some of the pieces of evidence the mayor and chancellor won't stop to look at.

Oregon's small-schools initiative was launched in 2004 with grants from the Gates Foundation and the Meyer Memorial Trust. Four years later, in 2008, after graduating their first class of students who had spent four years in intimate academies, the results indicated that "the small school experiment doesn't live up to hopes."[40]

A team of researchers from the New School's Center for New York City Affairs spent eighteen months studying data on small schools. What they concluded in their report, dated June 17, 2009, was that, "opening so many new schools caused collateral damage to existing large high schools as they absorbed the students displaced by closures of their large schools."[41] In an article by *Teachers College Record* in 2008, it was reported that the number of high schools nearly doubled in New York City as new small schools opened and large high schools were reorganized into smaller learning communities. They also found that unintended consequences of these new small schools may be the possibility that students left behind in large, established high schools were incurring negative impacts.[42] I myself saw these negative impacts when I was a mentor; regular high schoolers were rightfully jealous of all the new computers, new books, new furniture, new smart boards, and other new equipment that they saw being delivered only to the new mini school and not to their old school. Also, if small schools eventually promote higher achievement, many, many more will be needed to house the 91.5 percent of students still in large schools. As it is, many parents are complaining loudly that the small schools are crowding out the large high schools, taking over their art rooms and libraries.[43] The mayor doesn't pay attention to their concerns.

Financially, can we afford to create so many new small schools? *New York Teacher,* city edition, in an analysis of seven years of education spending in the Bloomberg administration, has found a number of changes in how dollars are allocated. There are now 1,075 more principals and assistant principals since Bloomberg took over, even as overall student enrollment has fallen, because the city has broken up underperforming schools into smaller ones. There are hundreds more schools (from 1,198 in 2002 to more than 1,500 now). New York City's education budget went from $11.5 billion in 2002 to $18.3 billion currently.[44] With debt and pension costs, it is really over $22 billion.

This increase reflects the central elements of the mayor's philosophy: smaller schools, relentless assessments of progress, and higher salaries for administrators. (John Dewey, one of the greatest education philosophers, is turning over in his grave.) "The spending pattern reflects the Bloomberg Administration's mindset that money attracts people who can bring business world success to the public arena. Mr. Klein has supported salaries reaching nearly $200,000 for several of his deputies and dozens of administrators who had little experience in public schools."[45] (Many came from careers in law or business.) Once again, we are confronted with business practices as the apex, the summit, the ultimate model, the highest point attainable, for educational practices!

The Bloomberg administration has been criticized for having too few educators control education policy. This lack of professionals is an enormous problem; it is like running a hospital without doctors. The researchers from the New School and others offered a note of caution for administrators concerning the opening of so many new schools. Do you think Bloomberg and Klein have listened and will be cautious? They have given no indication of caution so far; it is full speed ahead.

Herein lies another really big problem: Bloomberg and Klein rushed to implement the small-schools initiative without studying any sound research or past evidence of success (small schools had been tried before in New York City with poor results) and without testing it in just a few schools to see what works and what doesn't. Maybe rushing worked in business for them; after all, they are successful businessmen. But that rush has proved to be chaotic and destructive in New York City schools. Opening one hundred new small schools in the mayor's very first year of control, with the mayor's and the superintendent's lack of educational expertise and lack of consultation, was unsound, unrealistic, unprofessional, and doomed to failure. Professional educators and scientific education researchers would have known better than to rush to implement so many new schools all at once. According to Diane Ravitch, "No mayor has exercised such unlimited power over the public schools as Mr. Bloomberg. The Panel on Education Policy, the mayor's version of a school board, serves at the pleasure of the mayor and rubber stamps the policies and spending practices of the Department of Education, which is run by Mayor Bloomberg and Schools Chancellor Joel Klein."[46] Only once, at the beginning of the mayor's control, did two members on the panel dissent from the mayor's point of view. Mr. Bloomberg wanted to end what he called social promotion and install a new policy of leaving back huge numbers of students. Two board members cited research and proof that leaving back so many students was the wrong thing to do. So what did Mr. Bloomberg do? He fired the two dissenters and replaced them with two assenters; since that time no panel member has disagreed with the mayor on anything! "That's dangerous to democracy," says Diane Ravitch.[47] Is it any wonder that I fear for the demise of public education?

If you can still tolerate learning about more deceptive practices, I must tell you about charter schools because President Obama, as well as Mayor Bloomberg, has made the opening of more charter schools a big part of his plans for improving the nation's educational system. First, a little background: Since 1991, when the first charter school was opened in Minnesota, over 4,600 more have opened, and they now educate some 1.4 million of the nation's fifty million public school students.[48] The Obama administration has been working to persuade state legislators (who used to control education, right?) to lift the caps on the number of charter schools allowed. States, rightly so, have limited the number because of fear (now confirmed) of draining public school funds. (Charter schools are paid for with taxpayer money, unlike private schools; also, they operate free of many curricular regulations and union regulations that apply to traditional public schools.) Arne Duncan has said, "The charter school movement is one of the most profound changes in American education bringing tremendous new options to underserved communities."[49] Be skeptical—please!

In the Stanford University Study, as reported in the *New York Times*, June 22, 2009, the researchers in the Center for Research on Education Outcomes used student achievement data from fifteen states and the District of Columbia to gauge whether students who attended charter schools had fared better than they would have if they had attended a traditional public school.[50] Guess what? The report indicates that "nearly half of the charter schools nationwide have results that are no different from the local, public school options and over a third, 37 percent, deliver learning results that are *significantly worse*" (emphasis mine). "On average, students in charter schools seem to perform slightly worse than their peers in traditional public schools." (See Table 2, page 134.)[51]

Richard Iannuzzi, president of New York State United Teachers, has said, "Buffalo is a city where the dynamics of New York's charter school law play a significant role. Significant, it seems clear, not in supporting quality education, but in hampering it. The Buffalo city public schools have been financially crippled by the more than $71 million siphoned off to charter schools."[52] These schools in other cities have drawn millions of dollars in taxpayers' money away from traditional public schools, and most operate without union guidelines or union teachers.

There are some uninformed and unenlightened people who think that unions and union teachers are the problem in failing schools. If that were true, then these nonunion charter schools should be more successful, but they aren't. Ironically, unionized teachers are the only ones holding the line between chaos and stability and the total dismantling of public education. It is a fact that many successful charter schools are operated by the teachers' unions. In the education documentary *Waiting for Superman*, currently showing in theaters everywhere, Green Dot Charter School in the Bronx is highlighted as a high-performing charter school. Brent Staples, the editorial observer for the *New York Times*, in his October 2, 2010, article, "Waiting for Superman and the Education Debate" writes that the film's director, Davis Guggenheim, "did a serious disservice by not pointing out that these high-performing charter schools are fully unionized."[53] In addition, there are sixteen Green Dot charter schools in Los Angeles operated by the National Education Association, the largest teachers' union in the United States. What is really interesting, I think, is that Nelson Smith, president of the Charter School Alliance, in referring to the dismal results of the Stanford University study quoted above, said that he considered the Stanford Center, "a very reliable outfit and its director, Margaret Raymond, an esteemed researcher."[54] And he's president of the Charter School Alliance. What does that say about charter schools? This 2009 study, showing that charter school students slightly underperformed their traditional school peers in reading and math follows reports by the Rand Corporation in 2005 and the National Center for Educational Statistics in 2006 that also found charters not doing quite as well on average as district public schools. Mr. Duncan has seen these reports and has urged charter leaders to become more active in weeding out bad apples. Since Mr. Duncan seems to be relying on self-regulation and oversight, which didn't work in banking and didn't work on Wall Street and didn't work with British Petroleum, I don't think it will work here either, and there have been no signs of any "weeding out."

Charter schools were supposed to offer a better education for all children in the city's poor neighborhoods, but in New York City they have proportionally fewer Hispanic students as well as fewer students learning English than nearby schools, including schools that share the same building. Although Hispanics are the largest ethnic group in New York City's public schools, there are almost twice as many blacks among the thirty thousand charter school students. Also, on average, charter schools have fewer students who have limited English proficiency as well as fewer special education students.[55] Even with stacking the deck, charter schools do not perform as well as public schools.

Mayor Bloomberg wants to increase the number of charter schools—of course—in the city from one hundred to two hundred and the number of students in charter schools, now about thirty thousand, would increase to one hundred thousand by 2013.[56] The mayor would have to get the legislature to lift the current cap on the number of charter schools to get this feat accomplished. In addition, Mr. Bloomberg would have to have the state legislature give him the same power over charter schools that he has over the public schools. Since the mayor was able to pass two-term limit legislation at the beginning of his tenure and then overturn that law when he wanted three terms, getting the state lawmakers to give him power over charter schools doesn't look like it will be a problem. And it wasn't. Lo and behold, on Friday, May 28, 2010, "The New York Legislature voted to more than double the number of charter schools in the state. The measure would raise the maximum number to 460. In New York City, the number would be capped at 214."[57]

The new UFT president, Michael Mulgrew, said in a 2009 issue of New York Teacher that parents would find the mayor's plan to increase charter schools and increase services very "troubling" because the charter schools and their services will be at the expense of other public schools whose students, over 900,000, need these increased services just as much.[58] I wish Mr. Mulgrew would speak out more aggressively and defiantly; it wouldn't just be troubling—it would be a disaster. After all, he has the power to shut down every school. Since Mr. Bloomberg operates independently of the UFT and the parents and teachers of public school students, the mayor could very well get his way, wrong as it is. When I was a young teacher in the 1960s and the 1970s, drastic measures called strikes were used to halt the decline of the city schools, and they were effective. I think drastic measures are called for again. It remains to be seen if Mr. Mulgrew will demonstrate the strong leadership qualities of our very first union leader, the formidable Albert Shanker.

And now for the "pièce de résistance," otherwise known as the biggest tangled web of them all! After all the dismal reports and statistics and research and evidence that I have cited regarding the misleading, fraudulent, unreliable, and manipulated state standardized test scores, as well as the charter schools' unimpressive, lackluster performances, President Obama, along with his education secretary, Arne Duncan, is dangling $4.3 billion to those states who will rewrite education laws to open the door to more charter schools. "States that limit the growth of charter schools will have trouble getting an award," says Mr. Duncan.[59] Unbelievable! The $4.3 billion will also be used to expand the use of student standardized test scores (not even the gold standard NAEP tests) for judging teachers!

Now, the evaluation of teachers, based on these substandard, dumbeddown state test scores, is the cruelest joke of all. Even if the evaluation of teachers were based on NAEP test results, the gold standard tests, this method of evaluation would still be all wrong. If we were to judge dentists by the number of patients they treat who have healthy teeth, then the dentists in richer areas would always be judged superior, and the dentists in poorer areas, whose patients have poorer nutrition and poorer health care, including fewer dental visits, would always be judged inferior.

As in dentistry, so in education. Do all dentists get the same caliber of patients? Do all teachers get the same caliber of students? If President Obama is going to evaluate teachers by test scores, then every class should be statistically the same in terms of ability, behavior, language proficiency, parental support, family income, attendance, school environment, and health conditions. We know that low scores correlate with low income and that there are gross inequities in the quality of America's schools. Would it be fair to judge teachers, like dentists, by conditions beyond their control? Would it be fair to judge principals by conditions beyond their control? Read what happens when you do.

The *New York Times* reported on July 19, 2010, that a highly regarded Vermont principal of a high-poverty elementary school "was removed because the Burlington School District wanted to qualify for up to $3 million in federal stimulus money for its dozen schools."[60] Ms. Joyce Irvine was loved and revered by parents, students, faculty, superintendent, and State Senator Bernie Sanders. "Burlington is a major resettlement area and one recent September, 28 new students from Somalia,

Kenya, Ethiopia, Sudan arrived at Wheeler Elementary School and took the math test in October, only one month later."[61] About 115 of the 230 students at Wheeler are foreign-born, speak thirty different languages, are often traumatized, and have had little or no previous education. Yet, all students must take the reading test after only one year in the country.

Scores did go up—but not high enough or fast enough for federal stimulus money. Under Obama administration rules, such schools must either be replaced by a charter (Vermont has no charters) or have the principals removed and transform the schools. It doesn't matter that Ms. Irvine had already transformed the school!

Burlington was forced to remove Ms. Irvine in order to receive badly needed federal funds, "because performance evaluations based on test results . . . are a hallmark of the two main competitive grant programs the Obama administration developed to spur its initiatives, the stimulus and Race to the Top."[62] It doesn't matter that Wheeler Elementary School had a high poverty rate and large numbers of refugees: Only yearly test scores matter. The results are Kafkaesque, defying logic and common sense, and are another major political blunder in the guise of educational reforms.

Mr. Bloomberg announced on November 25, 2009, "that New York City public schools would immediately begin to use student test scores as a factor in deciding which teachers earn tenure."[63] (Never mind that it would be against the state law to do so; Mr. Bloomberg said that the law doesn't matter.) That means firing teachers whose students' test scores are low. If standardized test scores in math and reading will be tied in to evaluation, will the teachers of science and history and music and art (frivolous subjects?) not be evaluated? (Mr. Mulgrew, where are you?) The evaluation of teachers is extremely important and necessary; however, in no way should it be tied to test scores. It should be conducted by experienced, expert, educational supervisors, who are themselves master teachers and master trainers of teachers. These professional educational supervisors have to first train the teachers in the art and science of pedagogy before evaluation can or should be conducted.

Where are these educational supervisors who are master teachers and master trainers? Unfortunately, there are very few of them. They have been replaced by business people, lawyers, and other untrained noneducators. Only business people and other noneducators who have no knowledge of evidence-based educational practices, and no interest in seeking them out, like the mayor and the school chancellor and the president and the secretary of education, would call for linking teacher tenure to test scores. When I was mentoring, I met with the evaluators of my interns and to tell you the truth, most of them didn't know a good lesson when they saw it and certainly couldn't teach one themselves. If Duncan and Obama were professional educators, they never would have suggested spending over $4 billion of our money for results that not only will be fraudulent and deceptive but, even worse, won't provide the essential education America's students need and deserve.

Concerned citizens and other people who do pay attention to the well-publicized, evidence-based education reports were hoping that Mr. Obama's campaign rhetoric calling for an overhaul of NCLB would mean less federal control and less reliance on bogus state test scores. To our absolute dismay, this new stimulus package, called Race to the Top, makes testing even more important. Only some states will receive the funds, and with school budgets being slashed because of the weak economy, schools desperate for money will resort, once again, to devious practices. Race to the Top is a competition, a gamble, whereby some states will win large amounts of money and many others will not. How can we ever think of closing the achievement gap when the schools have been forced to enter a Las Vegas–type race that will result in winners and losers? I thought America wanted all its students to be winners, not just those who can run the fastest race. (Some states couldn't even enter the race, lacking resources to do so.) While there are always losers in Las Vegas, there should be none in education! Even NCLB, at least in title alone, recognized that all children should be helped to succeed. What a disgrace that this new educational plan is the best that President Obama has to offer us.

Unfortunately, there are still more problems that I must address. Arne Duncan has set the goal of closing and overhauling one thousand failed schools a year, nationwide, for the next five years—that's five thousand school closings. Congress has already appropriated $3 billion in the stimulus law to finance this effort.[64] Why the rush? Where is the evidence that this plan will work? Actually, there is no evidence of success, but there is evidence of failure.

When Arne Duncan was superintendent of Chicago public schools (2001–8), he presided over the closing of dozens of failing schools and is now drawing on those reforms to turn around the nation's schools. But a study by researchers at the University of Chicago has concluded "that most students who transferred out of closing schools re-enrolled in schools that were academically weak. Most students in schools that closed in the first five years of Mr. Duncan's tenure in Chicago saw little benefit."[65]

Well, where did Mr. Duncan expect these students from closed schools to go? The really good schools are filled to capacity; overcrowd them and they, too, decline. This problem has already occurred in some New York City schools. To use a current war cry, what is the exit strategy? Where will the students from the five thousand closed schools go? Doesn't anyone think A

HEAD?

The 2009 issue of *Education Next*, published by Harvard University, argues that school turnaround efforts have failed more often than not.[66]

As you can see, there are so many contradictory, manipulated reports on education practices today that spending billions of our dollars and rushing to make changes without a full understanding of all the problems and possible solutions is criminal in my mind. I had written a letter to Mr. Obama several months ago (no reply yet) asking him to convene, in Washington, a national education conference—actually a series of conferences, maybe months of conferences, however long it takes—at which professional educators, education research scientists, statisticians, state school superintendents, successful administrators, and teachers and parent association representatives from all across the country would discuss nothing less than the transformation of the schools. When Wall Street was in deep crisis, the president called in Wall Street specialists; when the banking industry was failing and collapsing, he called in bankers and financial experts. Whom did he call in to Washington to discuss the educational crisis? Anyone? Mayors and other concerned businessmen? Former professional basketball players, like Mr. Duncan?

President Obama needs to do for education what he has done for the war in Afghanistan. He had spent months meeting with the most knowledgeable people, including Secretary of Defense Robert Gates, Secretary of State Hillary Rodham Clinton, Joint Chiefs Chairman Admiral Mike Mullen, General David Petraeus, the late Special Envoy to Afghanistan and Pakistan Richard Holbrooke, former U.S. commander in Afghanistan General Stanley McChrystal, and scores of other professional people involved in the war. He reached a profoundly life-altering decision on whether to send more troops only after thorough, careful, deliberate debate and discussion with the best minds available. Well, nothing less will do for our troubled schools and America's schoolchildren. Before spending billions of dollars more, the American people need to know that the money to save the schools and give every student the opportunity to learn is really going to be used honestly and fairly, without subterfuge, outright cheating, and fraud. I hereby volunteer to be an active participant in this national educational "Call to Arms."

In this final chapter, I have repeatedly quoted from the *New York Times* to put together this fact-based case against the use and abuse of the states' standardized tests, charter schools, and the small–high school initiative. My initial intention was to write about my heroic Bronx students—I've told you that before—but the reader needs to know about the new obstacles urban students face if there is to be any chance of providing a sound education for them and for students across the country. I have relied a great deal on the *Times* because it is one of the very few remaining newspapers that report on national news, never mind educational news. (Murder, rape, other assorted crimes, sports, and entertainment dominate most newspapers.) But, I know that, obviously, many people don't pay attention to education news, and now I know that the editorial staff of the *New York Times* doesn't seem to pay attention to their own published educational news reports and studies. What else can I conclude after reading their editorial written on July 6, 2009, titled "Lessons for Failing Schools."[67] While acknowledging that 37 percent of charter schools offered a worse education than children would have received had they remained in traditional schools (and reporting on small schools' lack of success), they go on to agree with Mr. Duncan's plan to transform five thousand of the lowest-performing schools with "bold policies that have an impact right away." The editorial goes on to say that "states will need to shut down chronically failing schools and enroll students elsewhere."[68] Where? To small inefficient charter schools or small inefficient mini schools? Where oh where, Mr. Editor, do you plan to send thousands and thousands of students? Where is elsewhere? Over the rainbow?

Where is the money to build thousands of new small schools in the next few years, especially when the city school budget may be cut, because of the new economy, by $1 billion this year alone? Where are the professionally trained teachers and administrators to staff these schools?

And I must take issue with one more statement from this same July editorial: "The country needs bold action. It can no longer tolerate schools that have trapped generations of students at the margins of society and locked them out of the new economy."[69] Well, Mr. *New York Times* editor, look at this new economy based on greed and fraud; it has not only brought our mighty country down, but it has also widened the gap between the haves and the have-nots, increased the poverty rate, raised the unemployment rate to almost 10 percent, left millions of people homeless and hungry, without health care, and swindled and lied and cheated all of us ordinary citizens for the benefit of the very few, the very rich. Do you really want the next generation of young people to enter this new economy so that they can repeat the sins of their elders? To see how we treat our poorest students, go back to chapter 3 if you have forgotten and re-read my description of the decrepit state of Carter High School. Instead of building new schools, right here in New York City, Mayor Bloomberg has built two new billion-dollar baseball stadiums—where none were needed. The building of these stadiums shows what is truly valued; everything else is lip service.

This editorial does get one thing right. Turning around the most difficult schools will need an infusion of social services and community outreach programs that should be modeled on the highly successful Harlem Children's Zone in Manhattan. Instead of spending billions of dollars on the Race to the Top stimulus plan, that money, $4.3 billion, should be used to provide the services needed to emulate schools like the one in Harlem. We should be looking to study and emulate the success that is occurring elsewhere, in such places as Atlanta, Georgia, a big city with a large poor minority population that is having slow but steady success on the NAEP tests every year (see Table 3, "NAEP Statistics," page 135). What are they doing right? Why didn't the Broad Foundation give their $1 million award to a city that is legitimately improving, instead of granting it to New York City and Houston where the scores on NAEP tests were abysmal? The editorial staff of the New York Times and Mr. Broad and concerned citizens—pay attention. Your public schools are dying.

As President Franklin D. Roosevelt said, "The test of our progress is not whether we add more to the abundance of those who have much; it is whether we provide enough for those who have too little." We are failing this test. We are not making progress. Wake up, America.

As I conclude this last chapter, my usually optimistic outlook feels strained to its limits. New York City—the city in which I grew up, went to public school, and worked in for my whole life—New York State, our entire country, the world, seem to have so many overwhelming problems: war, famine, disease, poverty, global warming, environmental pollution, oil spill disasters—just an endless list of so many seemingly intractable problems. Who am I, a nobody, as I've told you, to think that an ordinary person can make a difference? Maybe there is nothing that can be done to fulfill the promise of America, to have an educated citizenry so that our government of, by, and for the people will not perish from the earth, corny as that may sound. How can we provide for the best education possible for all our young people, not just those in Scarsdale and Great Neck and at the Bronx High School of Science? My immigrant father, although retired and living on social security, spoke up every year in his Florida retirement community about the importance of passing the school budget. He would say, "You must pass it, even though we no longer have our own children in public school, because America's children are our children, our future." Am I losing my father's fighting spirit? Is everything hopeless and bleak?

Well, I just came back from a long break in writing this dismal chapter. I really was thinking of not finishing it. But, once again, I'm smiling, as I hear my father's voice and see his wise words stated above. I guess once an optimist, always an optimist, because during my break I sat down to read the newspaper and came across a 2009 article written by the *New York Times* columnist Bob Herbert, titled, "Changing the World."[70] Mr. Herbert has reminded me—what timing—about the brave individuals, such as Andrew Goodman, a young New York City college student who sacrificed his life to help Southern blacks get the vote in 1964. He also wrote about Rosa Parks, who refused to give up her seat on the bus to a white woman and thereby launched the Montgomery bus boycott, and so many other brave American souls who challenged America to do better and so it did. Thank you, Mr. Herbert, for reminding me that one person can make a difference, and everyone can try. We all have to try—maybe one at a time, maybe by the thousands, but we can make a difference and thereby change the world. We can untangle this terrible web of deceit that is being perpetrated in our schools all across America; we can stop the deception, dismantling, and demise of our schools. It can be done; there is still time. I still want to help.

P.S. If you want to fix the blame for the sorry state of our educational affairs, you can blame our politicians, ourselves for not being vigilant, local government, our state government, even our federal government. Whomever you blame, do not blame Bronx students because, despite all the obstacles we have put in their way, these amazing young people are definitely not *as bad as they say.*

Table 1. Some Harlem-Scarsdale gaps

	Harlem	Scarsdale
Median household income	$31,520	$166,906
Frequency of robberies as percentage of national average	214%	18%
Percent of adults with graduate degrees	13.3%	44.7%
Percent of students receiving free or reduced price lunches	78%	0
Percent black and Hispanic	96%	0
Per pupil expenditure	$17,857	$23,920
Average class size grade 8 math	27	19
Average SAT score—math	515 (all NYC)	655
Average SAT score—writing	492 (all NYC)	644
Four-year graduation rate	60%	99%

Source: *New York Teacher/City Edition*, October 15, 2009. By Maisie McAdoo.

Table 2. Comparison of performance on standardized tests: Charter school students versus public school students

	Reading		Math	
	Worse than public school peers	Better than public school peers	Worse than public school peers	Better than public school peers
National average	− 0.01*		− 0.03	
Arkansas		+ 0.02		+ 0.05
Arizona	− 0.01		− 0.04	
California		+ 0.02	− 0.03	
Colorado		+ 0.02		+ 0.07
District of Columbia	− 0.01			+ 0.01
Florida	− 0.02		− 0.03	
Georgia		+ 0.01	− 0.01	
Illinois		+ 0.00		+ 0.02
Louisiana		+ 0.06		+ 0.06
Minnesota	− 0.02		− 0.03	
Missouri		+ 0.03		+ 0.03
North Carolina		+ 0.01	− 0.03	
New Mexico	− 0.02		− 0.05	
Ohio	− 0.01		− 0.06	
Texas	− 0.05		− 0.05	

Source: Center for Research on Education Outcomes, Stanford University, *New York Times, June 22, 2009.*

* The numbers show differences in standardized test scores between charter school students and public school students, represented by standard deviation.

Table 3. Changes in NAEP reading scores

District	Grade 4		Grade 8	
	Since 2002	**Since 2005**	**Since 2002**	**Since 2005**
Atlanta	higher	higher	higher	higher
Austin	——*	no change**	——	no change**
Boston	——	no change**	——	no change**
Charlotte	——	no change**	——	no change**
Chicago	higher	no change**	no change**	no change**
Cleveland	——	no change**	——	higher
District of Columbia	higher	higher	no change**	higher
Houston	no change**	lower	no change**	higher
Los Angeles	no change**	no change**	higher	no change**
New York City	higher	no change**	***	no change**
San Diego	——	no change**	——	no change**

Source: National Cener for Education Statistics, U.S. Department of Education.

* ——indicates that the district did not participate in 2002.

** "no change" indicates that there was no significant change in the score in 2007.

*** Reporting standards not met. Sample size was insufficient to permit a reliable estimate for New York City in 2002.

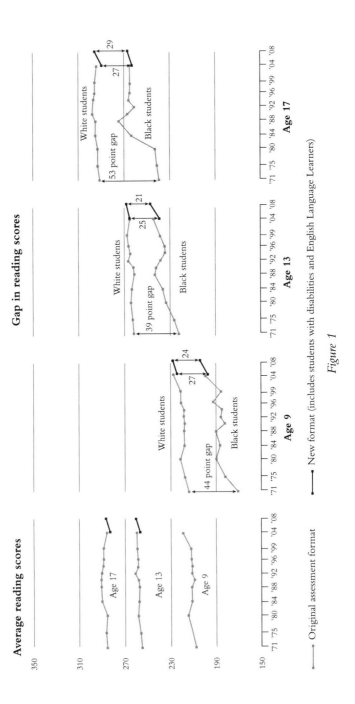

Figure 1

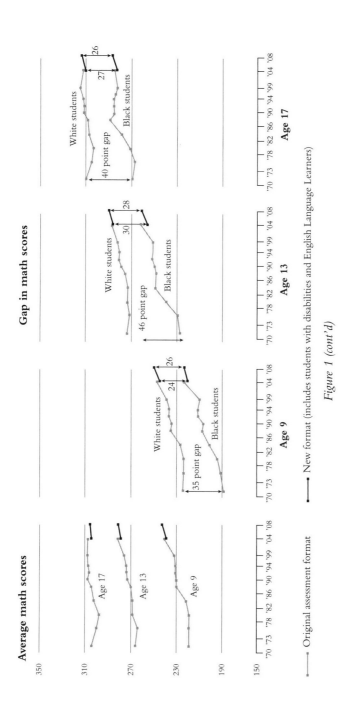

Figure 1 (cont'd)

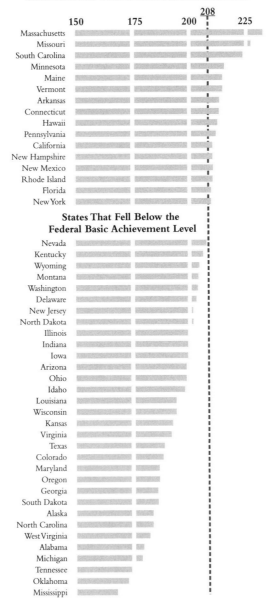

Figure 2

Percentage of students who passed state exams

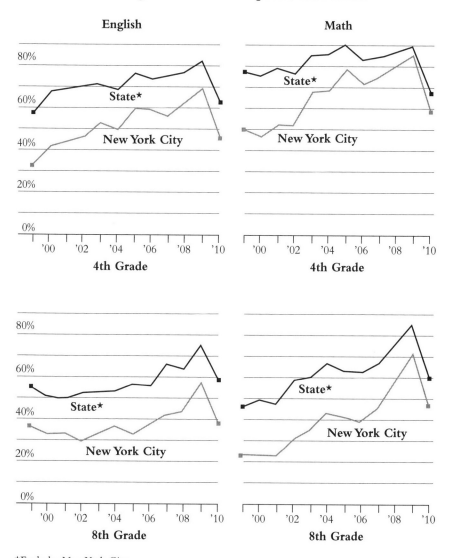

English

Math

4th Grade

4th Grade

8th Grade

8th Grade

*Excludes New York City

Figure 3

Janet,
you've become
one of the most
important people in
all my learning life.
Thank you for the
inspiration. Love Trina

Janet –
you are so amazing and were
my inspiration this whole year.
you can never let that lead enough!
love, Erin

Janet –
Honestly, I never
could have done it
without you.
Thank you for everything!

Love
Abby

Janet,
Your help was
invaluable. For
your encouragement,
humor, suggestions,
and availability,
I'm indebted.
Jerome

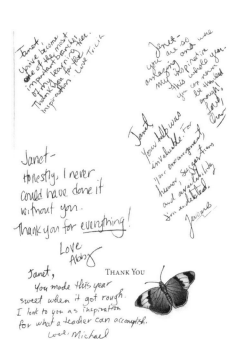

Janet,
You made this year
sweet when it got rough.
I look to you as inspiration
for what a teacher can accomplish.
Love, Michael

THANK YOU

Janet
thanks to you
I stuck through
this challenging year!
you are the sweetest
person I've ever met!
Thank you so much!
Perla

Dear Janet,

I know you already know this, but you are an incredibly special person! I am so thankful that you were there to help me get through the first year of teaching. None of your "interns" could have made it through this first year in one piece without your constant support, advice, cheerfullness, optimism, materials, sympathy, knowledge, (over) patience, mid-term grading ability, dragon-lady-fighting skills, everything! The Board of Ed doesn't know how lucky it's been all these years to have you. Much love and thanks,

Chava

Appendixes

Appendix A
Letter from M. Rasool

Reprinted with permission of M. Rasool, South African teacher

4 November 1994

Dear Janet,

I have been informed by the American Federation of Teachers that you and your class have been matched in the Classroom-to-Classroom programme with myself. For both my students and myself, it is indeed a real pleasure to forge new relations with fellow colleagues in the USA.

Before I begin the task of discussing the programme itself, I think it would be appropriate for me to tell you something about South Africa and its people.

I am sure that you have already learnt that South Africa has finally rid itself of the shackles of apartheid (racial segregation) with the holding of non-racial, democratic elections for the first time in its history this year. We now have a non-racial, democratic government and constitution in place at the political level. However, the country is still a deeply divided one with many of the old apartheid structures and practices still in place. The white minority continue to reap the benefits of the economy. In addition, although the new government has committed itself to de-racialising the education system, separate schools for whites and blacks remain. On a more positive side, the process of social South Africa rids itself of the remaining vestiges of apartheid. After all, societal transformation is not something that occurs overnight. There is also a feeling of national reconciliation and forgiveness that is running through the hearts and souls of most South Africans—no better typified than in the character of our state president—Nelson Mandela. This is good and remarkable in view of the horrors that we black South Africans have been subjected to under centuries of apartheid rule (or misrule). We South Africans are fast learning to forgive and forget.

I live in the region (province) of KwaZulu/Natal. The area has a cosmopolitan population (like the rest of SA) but the majority of people are of the Zulu indigenous group. I am of Indian descent—my forefathers came to SA in the 1860s to work as laborers in the sugar plantations of the then British Colony of Natal. I live in the resort city of Durban along the east coast of SA. It is small by New York standards, but large by South African standards.

As I mentioned earlier, education in SA is still racially divided. Historically, education has been segregated into 4 compartments: White, Indian, Coloured (mixed race) and African. The White group has received the best education funding—they have the best resourced schools, highly qualified teachers and the best opportunities for moving into tertiary education and high paying jobs. On the other hand, African education is the worst off: poorly resourced schools, lowly qualified teachers, lack of provision, etc. I must admit that Indians and Coloureds, although, part of the historically oppressed group, have had marginally better treatment in comparison to their African counterparts.

Therefore provision of education for Indians is somewhere between black and white education. This was the nature of apartheid, to divide the oppressed so that they would keep on fighting with each other instead of attacking the source of oppression.

As I mentioned earlier, moves are afoot to deracialise education and we can expect to be teaching in racially mixed classrooms in the foreseeable future. This is going to be a real challenge for teachers, since pupils will be coming from different backgrounds—either historically advantaged or disadvantaged.

I teach in a formerly Indian residential area of Phoenix. This is a township with a population of about 300,000 people—it is about 25 kilometres from my home which happens to be near the CBD. Phoenix is an area which houses the lower socio-economic group in the Indian community (in general most Indians have done well in South Africa). I would imagine that this area is no different from other such areas in the rest of the world. Unemployment and alcoholism is rife, not to mention drug abuse. Since a number of children come from troubled homes, these problems tend to infiltrate the school set up. No doubt, the problematic backgrounds of a number of my pupils have affected their interest in school and performances adversely. There are, of course, a number of pupils who do come from stable homes and tend to perform better. You will gather by now that I am teaching in an environment where the social ills of society have been placed on the doorstep of the classroom. There are, of course, many "first world" types of schools in Durban but I prefer working in this environment—it gives me a great deal of satisfaction to see if these are the problems of Indian children, can you imagine those of African children who were most disadvantaged under apartheid?

I teach history at grades 10, 11, 12 although I also take classes at junior secondary. By the time you would have received this letter, our pupils would have begun their final examinations and the year would be almost ended (that is, academic year). I am therefore hoping that our exchanges would benefit in the 1995 academic year. I am particularly interested in 20th Century world history—which, in essence, is the matric (grade 12) syllabus.

We teach themes like:

The rise of the superpowers
The events leading to the Second World War
The Cold War in Europe, South East Asia, Africa
and the Middle East and Latin America.

Be warned that the discipline/subject of History is a particularly heated issue in our country. In South Africa the teaching of History under apartheid was nothing but propaganda reminiscent of the Hitlerian Era. Syllabi, riven with inconsistencies, falsehoods and blatant lies were drawn up by the grand masters of apartheid (the ruling minority) with the sole intention of justifying white minority rule—in short, it was an interpretation of life from the perspective of white historians. Teachers were compelled to teach the authorised syllabus, any deviation from this was regarded as subversive and such teachers were labeled as trouble-makers. (If you see the movie *Sarafina* it would give you a good idea of teaching under apartheid rule.)

Over the last few years various stakeholders in education having been reconstructing the curriculum. Therefore we history teachers are expecting new syllabi to be made available next year reflecting a more accurate version of our history. We are also hoping that previously banned material would be made available more freely in future.

The problem is that under apartheid, there was no semblance of a normal school life. Political violence, state harassment, poverty and other social ills have ensured that the academic development of black children remain retarded. However, with the inauguration of a democratic order in South Africa, teachers have the mighty task of uplifting disadvantaged children from formerly disenfranchised communities. With this in mind, I am sure that your students and yourself will understand and accept the many shortcomings of my pupils brought on by 300 years of systematic racial persecution.

I think that I have burdened you with enough reading already. There is so much more that I would like to tell you about life in South Africa—but it is not possible in one letter.

Is your school the typical school in the Bronx that we so often see in the movies? In my next letter I will tell you more about myself—something I forgot to mention in this letter.

Hoping to hear from you soon.

Yours faithfully

s/M. Rasool

Appendix B
Course of Study for Multicultural Literature

Note: I have indicated in parentheses the author's country of origin, or, in the case of American writers, their culture or ethnicity. Not all books were read in their entirety. Excerpts were used frequently; however, students often chose to read the entire book either for extra credit, or for their book report, or in many cases, they read the entire book just because they loved it. Eureka!

African American Literature

Earliest Slave Literature

Douglass, Frederick. *Narrative of the Life of Frederick Douglass, An American Slave*. In *Early African American Classics*, edited by Anthony Appiah. New York: Bantam Books, 1990.

Du Bois, W. E. B. *The Souls of Black Folk*. In *Early African American Classics*, edited by Anthony Appiah. New York: Bantam Books, 1990.

Jacobs, Harriet. *Incidents in the Life of a Slave Girl, Written by Herself*. In *Early African American Classics*, edited by Anthony Appiah. New York: Bantam Books, 1990.

Johnson, James Weldon. *The Autobiography of an Ex-colored Man*. In *Early African American Classics*, edited by Anthony Appiah. New York: Bantam Books, 1990.

Washington, Booker T. *Up from Slavery*. In *Early African American Classics*, edited by Anthony Appiah. New York: Bantam Books, 1990.

Books

Angelou, Maya. *I Know Why The Caged Bird Sings*. New York: Bantam Books, 1971.
Baldwin, James. *The Fire Next Time*. New York: Vintage Books, 1963.
————. *Nobody Knows My Name*. New York: Dell, 1961
————. *Notes of a Native Son*. Boston: Beacon Press, 1955.
Haley, Alex. *The Autobiography of Malcolm X*. New York: Ballantine, 1973.
————. *Roots*. Garden City, N.Y.: Doubleday, 1976.
Hurston, Zora Neale. *Their Eyes Were Watching God*. New York: Harper Collins, 2000.
Mathabane, Mark. *Kaffir Boy*. New York: Free Press, 1998.
————. *Love in Black and White*. New York: Harper Collins, 1992.
Morrison, Toni. *Beloved*. New York: Alfred A. Knopf, 1987.
————. *The Bluest Eye*. New York: Plume Books, 1994.
Walker, Alice. *The Color Purple*. New York: Pocket Books, 1982.
————. *Possessing the Secret of Joy*. New York: Harcourt Brace Jovanovich, 1992.
————. *In Search of Our Mother's Gardens*. New York: Harcourt Brace Jovanovich, 1984.
Wright, Richard. *Black Boy*. New York: Harper Collins, 1993.

Poems

Angelou, Maya. *Poems*. New York: Bantam Books, 1981.
————. "The Pulse of Morning" (poem written for President Clinton's inauguration). In *Celebrations: Rituals of Peace and Prayer*. New York: Random House, 2006.
Baraka, Amiri (formerly known as LeRoi Jones). Selected poems. In *African American Poetry*, edited by Virginia Seeley. Englewood Cliffs, N.J.: Globe Books, 1993.
Brooks, Gwendolyn. Selected poems. In *Heath Anthology of American Literature*, edited by Paul Lauter, vol. 2. Lexington, Mass.: Houghton Mifflin, 1994.
Dove, Rita. Selected poems. In *Heath Anthology of American Literature*, edited by Paul Lauter, vol. 2. Lexington, Mass.: Houghton Mifflin, 1994.
Giovanni, Nikki. Selected poems. In *African American Poetry*, edited by Virginia Seeley. Englewood Cliffs, N.J.: Globe Books, 1993.

Hughes, Langston. Selected poems. In *Heath Anthology of American Literature*, edited by Paul Lauter, vol. 2. Lexington, Mass.: Houghton Mifflin, 1994.

Plays

Hansberry, Lorraine. *A Raisin in the Sun*. In *Four Contemporary Plays*, edited by Bennett Cerf. New York: Vintage Books, 1961.

Wilson, August. *Fences*. New York: Plume Books, 1986.

Spanish, Hispanic, Latino/Latina, Caribbean Writers

Books

Alvarez, Julia. *How The Garcia Girls Lost Their Accents*. New York: Penguin, 1992. (Dominican Republic)

Cervantes Saavedra, Miguel de. *Don Quixote de La Mancha*. New York: AMS Press, 1967. (Spain)

Cisneros, Sandra. *The House on Mango Street*. New York: Vintage Books, 1989. (Mexican American)

Danticat, Edwidge. *Krik? Krak!* New York: Vintage Books, 1996. (Haiti)

Ferré, Rosario. *Pandora's Papers*. New York: Vintage Books, 1976. (Puerto Rico)

————. *The Youngest Doll*. In *Multicultural Perspectives*, by David W. Foote, Arthur N. Applebee, Judith A. Langer, et al. Evanston, Ill.: McDougal, Littell, 1993.

Garcia Márquez, Gabriel. *Innocent Eréndira and Selected Short Stories*. New York: Harper and Row, 1978. (Colombia)

Love in the Time of Cholera. New York: Vintage Books, 1988.

————. *One Hundred Years of Solitude*. New York: Harper Perennial, 1970.

Hijuelos, Oscar. *The Mambo Kings Play Songs of Love*. New York: Harper & Row, 1989. (Cuba)

Kincaid, Jamaica. *Annie John*. New York: New American Library, 1983. (West Indies)

Menchú, Rigoberto. *I, Rigoberto Menchú: An Indian Woman in Guatemala*. New York: Verso, 1984. (Guatemala)

Rodriguez, Richard. *Hunger of Memory*. New York: Dial, 2004 (Mexican American)

Santiago, Esmeralda. *When I Was Puerto Rican*. New York: Addison-Wesley, 1993. (Puerto Rico)

Selected Poems

Laviera, Tato. Selected poems. In *Heath Anthology of American Literature*, edited by Paul Lauter, vol. 2. Lexington, Mass.: Houghton Mifflin, 1994. (Puerto Rico)

McKay, Claude. Selected poems. In *Multicultural Perspectives*, by David W. Foote, Arthur N. Applebee, Judith Langer, et al. Evanston, Ill.: McDougal, Littell, 1993. (Jamaica)

Mistral, Gabriela. *Selected Poems of Gabriela Mistral*. Albuquerque: University of New Mexico Press, 2003. (Chile)

Neruda, Pablo. Selected poems. In *Multicultural Perspectives*, by David W. Foote, Arthur N. Applebee, Judith Langer, et al. Evanston, Ill.: McDougal, Littell, 1993. (Chile)

Rodríguez de Tió, Lola. Selected poems. In *An Anthology of Puerto Rican Literature*. New York: Vintage, 1974. (Puerto Rico)

Soto, Gary. Selected poems. In *Multicultural Perspectives*, by David W. Foote, Arthur N. Applebee, Judith Langer, et al. Evanston, Ill.: McDougal, Littell, 1993. (Mexican American)

Native American Literature

Folklore

Selected tales. In Robert Dolezal's *American Folklore and Legend Anthology*. Pleasantville, N.Y.: Readers Digest, 1981.

Books

Brown, Dee. *Bury My Heart at Wounded Knee*. New York: Bantam Books, 1972.

Carter, Forrest (Asa). *The Education of Little Tree*. Albuquerque: University of New Mexico Press, 1985.

Dorris, Michael. *The Broken Cord*. New York: Harper Perennial, 1989.

Erdrich, Louise. *Love Medicine*. New York: Bantam Books, 1984.

Momaday, N. Scott. *House Made of Dawn*. New York: Harper and Row, 1966.

Silko, Leslie Marmon. *Ceremony*. New York: Penguin, 1986.

Poems

Silko, Leslie Marmon. *Laguna Woman Poems*. Greenfield Center, N.Y.: Greenfield Review Press, 1974.

Asian Literature

Hayslip, Le Ly. *When Heaven and Earth Changed Places*. New York: Penguin Group, 1990. (Vietnam)

Hosseini, Khaled. *The Kite Runner*. New York: Riverhead Books, 2003. (Afghanistan)★

Mahfouz, Naguib. *Palace Walk*. New York: Doubleday, 1990. (Egypt)

Mishima, Yukio. *Death in Midsummer and Other Stories*. New York: New Directions, 1966. (Japan)

Nafisi, Azar. *Reading Lolita in Tehran*. New York: Random House, 2003. (Iran)★

Tan, Amy. *The Joy Luck Club*. New York: Random House, 1989. (Chinese American)

———. The Kitchen God's Wife. New York: G. P. Putnam's Sons, 1991. (Chinese American)

Yoshiko. *Journey to Topaz*. Berkeley, Calif.: Creative Arts, 1988. (Japanese American)

★I added the titles with asterisks to the list when I was a mentor in Bronx high schools from 2003 to 2005.

Jewish Writers

Fiction

Ozick, Cynthia. *The Shawl*. New York: Alfred A. Knopf, 1989.

Ross, Leonard Q. *The Education of Hyman Kaplan*. Orlando: Harcourt Brace, 1937.

Nonfiction

Keneally, Thomas. *Schindler's List*. New York: Simon and Schuster, 1982.

Spiegelman, Art. *Maus I: A Survivor's Tale: My Father Bleeds History*. New York: Pantheon Books, 1973. (graphic format)

———. *Maus II : A Survivor's Tale: And Here My Troubles Began*. New York: Pantheon Books, 1991. (graphic format)

Wiesel, Elie. *All Rivers Run to the Sea*. New York: Alfred A. Knopf, 1995.

———. *Night*. New York: Bantam Books, 1982.

Appendix C
Interest Inventory

Directions: Answer the following questions using complete sentences. (Teacher reads questions to students)

1. What is your full name, age, and birthday?
2. Where were you born?
3. How many brothers and/or sisters do you have?
4. What schools have you attended—beginning with elementary school?
5. Which school was your favorite? Why?
6. Which school was your least favorite? Why?
7. What is/are your favorite subject(s)?
8. What is/are your least favorite subject(s)?
9. What are your favorite television shows?
10. What are your favorite movies? Favorite movie stars?
11. What kind of music do you like? (rock, rap, hip-hop, jazz, country, etc.)
12. Who are your favorite singers and or groups?
13. What are your favorite sports?
14. What are your favorite teams? Favorite players?
15. Do you participate in any sports? Which one(s)?
16. What are your favorite magazines, books, and/or stories?
17. What are your hobbies outside of school?
18. What are your plans and dreams for the future? (after graduation from high school)

Notes

1. Introduction

1. David M. Herszenhorn, "School Financing Case Plays Out in Court," *New York Times*, 10 October 2006, B1.

2. Ibid.

3. David M. Herszenhorn, "N.Y. Courts Cut Aid Sought by City Schools," *New York Times*, 21 November 2006, A1.

4. Ibid.

5. See http://www.ed.gov/nclb/overview/intro/factsheet.html.

6. See www.publicschoolreview.com (Scarsdale).

7. See http://www.antonnews.com/greatneckrecord/news.html.

8. Jonathan Kozol, *The Shame of the Nation: The Restoration of Apartheid Schooling in America* (New York: Crown Publishers, 2005).

2. Nobody

1. I'm nobody. Who are you?
   Are you nobody, too?
   Then there's a pair of us—don't tell.
   They'd banish us, you know.
   How dreary to be somebody.
   How public, like a frog
   To tell your name the livelong June
   To an admiring bog.

From Emily Dickinson, "I'm Nobody," in *The American Tradition in Literature,* vol. 2, ed. S. Bradley (New York: Grosset and Dunlap, 1967), 181.

2. Mark Seidenberg, "Taking Educational Research to School," *Science* (11 September 2009): 1340.

3. See www2.ed.gov/news/staff/bios/duncan.html.

4. There is no frigate like a book
   To take us lands away,
   Nor any coursers like a page of prancing poetry.
   This traverse may the poorest take
   Without oppress of toil;
   How frugal is the chariot
   That bears a human soul.

From Emily Dickinson, "No Frigate Like a Book," in *My American Heritage*, collected by R. Henry (New York: Rand McNally, 1949), 145.

5. Neil Postman and Charles Weingartner, *Teaching as a Subversive Activity* (New York: Dell, 1969), xiii.

6. Ibid., 2.

7. Ibid., xiii.

8. More quotations from *Teaching as a Subversive Activity*:

"If your goals are to make people more alike and prepare them to be docile functionaries in some bureaucracy and prevent them from being vigorous-self-directed learners, then our present all consuming national and state standardized testing is the right curriculum" (67).

"These standardized tests devalue, even denigrate, the uniqueness of each learner's perception" (92).

"Knowledge is an outcome of perception and is as unique and subjective as any other perception. Knowledge is what we have after we have learned" (92).

"We see things not as they are, but as we are" (98).

"Any talk about high standards from teachers or administrators . . . is nonsense unless they are talking about standards of learning as distinct from standards for grades" (67).

"What is it that this organism needs without which he cannot thrive?
a. the need for people
b. need for good communication with other people
c. need for a loving relationship with other people
d. need for a workable concept of self
e. need for freedom
   Build a curriculum around these ideas and "they will come" (68).

9. J. Abner Peddiwell, *The Saber-Tooth Curriculum: A Satire on American Education* (New York: McGraw-Hill, 1939), 44.

3. It Was the Worst of Times

1. See http:www.nyTimes.com/2006112/311ny region/default.html.

2. "Tabloid Headlines, 'FORD TO CITY: DROP DEAD,'" The Big Apple—A Website by Barry Popik (www.barrypopik.com/index.php/new_york_city/entry/tabloid_headlines_ford_to_city).

3. http://mets2006.wordpress.com/2008/09/26/armageddon-al-shanker-saved-the-city-in-1975

4. See http://www.advocatesforchildren.org/pubs/hsnsurvey/page 7.html.

5. See http://nyc.gov/html/records/htm/collections/education/1130.

6. Elyssa Ely, M.D., "How Dust Yields Clue to Asthma," *New York Times*, 7 April 2009, D5.

7. Ibid.

8. See http://www.nycares.org/volunteer/annual_events/nycd/index.php.

9. Lorraine Hansberry, *A Raisin in the Sun*, in *Four Contemporary American Plays*, ed. Bennett Cerf (New York: Random House, 1961), 205.

6. Marion—A Rare Gem

1. Jonathan Kozol, *The Shame of the Nation: The Restoration of Apartheid Schooling in America* (New York: Crown Publishers, 2005).

9. Multiple Intelligences: A Digression

1. Howard Gardner, "Probing More Deeply into the Theory of Multiple Intelligences," *Bulletin of the National Association of Secondary School Principals* 80, no. 583 (1996): 4.

2. Thomas R. Hoerr, "Introducing the Theory of Multiple Intelligences," *Bulletin of the National Association of Secondary School Principals* 80, no. 583 (1996): 9–10.

3. Howard Gardner, *Multiple Intelligences: The Theory in Practice* (New York: Basic Books, 1993), 12.

4. Ibid., 9.

5. Ibid., 8.

6. Sam Dillon, "Schools Slow in Closing Gaps between Races," *New York Times*, 20 November 2006, A18.

7. Gardner, *Multiple Intelligences*, 11.

10. Dolores—The Dancer

1. Howard Gardner, *Multiple Intelligences: The Theory in Practice* (New York: Basic Books, 1993), 47.

2. Sam Roberts, "City Poverty Rate Dipped in 2008, New Census Data Show," *New York Times*, 29 September 2009, A31.

12. Pedro—The Piano Player

1. Joseph W. Gauld, "Meeting Each Student's Unique Potential: One Approach to Education," *Bulletin of the National Association of Secondary School Principals* 80, no. 583 (1996): 43.

14. Deception, Dismantling, and Demise of Public Education

1. Michael Dobbs, "Education 'Miracle' Has a Math Problem," *Washington Post*, 8 November 2003.
2. Ibid.
3. Ibid.
4. Ibid.
5. Ibid.
6. Ibid.
7. Ibid.
8. See www2.ed.gov/policy/elsec/leg/esea02/index.html.
9. Maisie McAdoo, "Some Harlem Scarsdale Gaps," *New York Teacher*, city edition, L1, no. 3 (2009): 11.
10. See www2.ed.gov/policy/elsec/leg/esea02/index.html.
11. Sam Dillon, "Federal Researchers Find Lower Standards in Schools," *New York Times*, 30 October 2009, 22.
12. National Center for Educational Statistics, U.S. Department of Education.
13. Sam Dillon, "Sluggish Results Seen in Math Scores," *New York Times*, 15 October 2009, A18.
14. Sam Dillon, "'No Child' Law Is Not Closing a Racial Gap in Scores, Tests Show," *New York Times*, 29 April 2009, A1, A16.
15. Dillon, "Federal Researchers Find Lower Standards."
16. Dillon, "'No Child' Law Is Not Closing a Racial Gap."
17. Javier Hernandez, "Botched Most Answers on New York State Math Test? You Still Pass," *New York Times*, 14 September 2009, A14.
18. Jennifer Medina, "As Many Schools Earn A's and B's, City Plans to Raise Standards," *New York Times*, 4 September 2009, A18.
19. Ibid.
20. Sharon Otterman and Robert Gebeloff, "With Standards Tightened, Far Fewer New York City Schools Receive a Grade of 'A,'" *New York Times*, 1 October 2010, A21.
21. Jennifer Medina, "With Teachers' Contract to End, Talks Are Quiet," *New York Times*, 30 October 2009, A25.
22. http://www.broadfoundation.org/about_broads.html
23. Diane Ravitch, "Mayor Bloomberg's Crib Sheet," *New York Times*, 9 April 2009, op ed.

24. Meredith Kolodner, "Mayor Bloomberg's Boast on Graduation Rates Is Misleading, According to Study," *New York Daily News*, 23 September 2009.

25. Jennifer Medina, "U.S. Math Test Finds Scant Gains," *New York Times*, 14 October 2009.

26. Ibid.

27. Ravitch, "Mayor Bloomberg's Crib Sheet."

28. "Democrats and Poor Kids," editorial, *Wall Street Journal*, 6 April 2009, A14.

29. Dillon, "Federal Researchers Find Lower Standards."

30. Shaila Dewan, "Georgia Schools Inquiry Finds Signs of Cheating," *New York Times*, 12 February 2010.

31. Sharon Otterman and Jennifer Medina, "Klein Resigning as Chancellor City Schools." *New York Times*, 10 November 2010, A1, A28.

32. David Chen and Michael Barbaro, "Mayor's Search Method: Stay within the Circle," *New York Times*, 11 November, A1, A32.

33. Ibid.

34. Elissa Gootman and Jennifer Medina, "No Education Experience Needed to Run Schools? An Idea Is Taken to a New Level, *New York Times*, 11 November 2010, A32.

35. Diane Ravitch, *The Death and Life of the Great American School System* (New York: Basic Books, 2010), 82.

36. American Youth Policy Forum, "Trip Report: Small High Schools and Early/Middle College High School, New York City, NY," www.aypf.org, 2004.

37. Michael Winerip, "A Chosen Few Are Teaching for America," *New York Times*, 12 July 2010, A10, A13.

38. Javier Hernandez, "Study Cites Dire Economic Impact of Poor Schools," *New York Times*, 23 April 2009, A22.

39. Betsy Hammond and Lisa Grace Lednicer, "Small School Experiment Doesn't Live Up to Hopes," Newhouse News Service, 23 June 2008.

40. Ibid.

41. www.newschool.edu/milano/nycaffairs/documents/TheNewMarket place_Report.pdf.

42. See www.tcrecord.org/content.asp?contentid=15169.

43. Jennifer Medina, "City's Schools Share Their Space, and Bitterness," *New York Times*, 30 November 2009, A1.

44. Maisie McAdoo, "The School System under Mayoral Control—Then and Now," *New York Teacher*, city edition (September 2009): 6.

45. Jennifer Medina and Robert Gebeloff, "With More Money, City Schools Add Jobs, Many at Top Dollar," *New York Times*, 1 July 2009, A1, A30.

46. Ravitch, "Mayor Bloomberg's Crib Sheet," *New York Times*, 9 April 2009.

47. Elizabeth Green, "Feud 'twixt Wylde, Ravitch, Laid to City's Machinations," *New York Sun*, 31 August 2007.

48. Sam Dillon, "Education Chief to Warn Advocates That Inferior Charter Schools Harm the Effort," *New York Times*, 22 June 2009, A10.

49. Ibid.

50. Ibid.

51. Ibid.

52. Richard Iannuzzi, "Budget Politics, Promising Programs Affect Quality," *New York Teacher*, state edition, 26 November 2009, 10.

53. Brent Staples, "Waiting for Superman and the Education Debate," *New York Times*, 2 October 2010, A18.

54. Dillon, "Education Chief to Warn Advocates That Inferior Charter Schools Harm the Effort."

55. Jennifer Medina and Robert Gebeloff, "New York Charter Schools Lag in Enrolling Hispanics," *New York Times*, 15 June 2010, A23, A27.

56. Jennifer Medina, "New York State Votes to Double Charter Schools," *New York Times*, 29 May 2010, A1, A20.

57. Ibid.

58. Dorothy Callace, "Mayor's Charter Plan Not for All Kids," *New York Teacher* 11, no. 3, (2009).

59. Sam Dillon, "Dangling $4.3 Billion, President Pushes States to Shift on Education," *New York Times*, 17 August 2009, A1, A10.

60. Michael Winerip, "A Highly Regarded Principal Wounded by Good Intentions," *New York Times*, 19 July 2010, A11.

61. Ibid.

62. Ibid.

63. Jennifer Medina, "Mayor to Link Teacher Tenure to Test Scores," *New York Times*, 25 November 2009, A1.

64. Sam Dillon, "Report Questions Duncan's Policy of Closing Failing Schools," *New York Times*, 29 October 2009, A17.

65. Ibid.

66. Ibid.

67. "Lessons for Failing Schools," editorial, *New York Times*, 6 July 2009, A18.

68. Ibid.

69. Ibid.

70. Bob Herbert, "Changing the World," *New York Times*, 27 October 2009, A31.

Index